Praise for
Celebrations That Touch the Heart

"Parents should wear out this creative resource! It's filled with ideas that promote spiritual growth, are fun, and don't require a second mortgage to implement. But I won't stick Brenda's book on my kids-only shelf. Her ideas are broader than that. I can hardly wait to use some with my church home group."

—MARLENE LeFEVER, author of *Parties with a Purpose,*
Learning Styles, and *Creative Teaching Methods*

"Brenda Poinsett has a winsome way of inspiring people to celebrate in extraordinary ways. Her suggestions are not only simple and affordable, they are also fun and instructive. *Celebrations That Touch the Heart* will motivate you to add a spiritual dimension to *all* your family and holiday celebrations."

—DOROTHY KELLEY PATTERSON, general editor of *The Woman's*
Study Bible, author of *BeAttitudes for Women, A Woman*
Seeking God, and *Where's Mom?*

"Brenda reminds us of what truly matters in our work and lives. It is vital to well-being that we find time and space to create moments of meaning with those we love. A remarkable book!"

—MARK LeBLANC, SmallBusinessSuccess.com
and author of *Growing Your Business!*

"Whether she's talking about creating new family traditions or spicing up existing ones, Brenda Poinsett offers us insights about the history and spiritual significance of many of our holidays. Thank you, Brenda, for giving me ideas about how to celebrate creatively and to share my Christian faith with family and friends during holidays."

—HEATHER KING, Women's Ministry Director,
State Convention of Baptists in Indiana

"Brenda Poinsett's creative approach to family celebrations comes alive in *Celebrations That Touch The Heart*. Now her celebration designs are available for parents, grandparents, teachers, and professional church educators who want to create special memories for families. This book will be a great addition to family and church libraries."

—CEDRIC C. COX, director of Educational Ministries for
American Baptist Churches of Indiana and Kentucky

"Two of the most magical words in any child's vocabulary are *we always*. In a world where nothing seems to stay the same, establishing family traditions is a powerful life-affirming tool. Brenda Poinsett has put together a wonderful guide for parents who want to cultivate family unity and identity. If you want your children to grow up saying 'We always celebrate with Jesus,' then *Celebrations That Touch the Heart* is just for you."

—DONNA PARTOW, author of *Becoming A Vessel God Can Use*

CELEBRATIONS

THAT TOUCH THE HEART

CELEBRATIONS
THAT TOUCH THE HEART

Creative Ideas
to Make Your Holidays
and Special Events
Meaningful

Brenda Poinsett

WATERBROOK
PRESS

CELEBRATIONS THAT TOUCH THE HEART
PUBLISHED BY WATERBROOK PRESS
2375 Telstar Drive, Suite 160
Colorado Springs, Colorado 80920
A division of Random House, Inc.

All scripture quotations, unless otherwise indicated, are taken from the *King James Version*. Scripture quotations marked (TLB) are taken from *The Living Bible* copyright © 1971. Used by permission of Tyndale House Publishers, Inc., Wheaton, Illinois 60189. All rights reserved. Scripture quotations marked (NIV) are taken from the *Holy Bible, New International Version*®. NIV®. Copyright © 1973, 1978, 1984 by International Bible Society. Used by permission of Zondervan Publishing House. All rights reserved. Scripture quotations marked (TEV) are from the *Today's English Version*—Second Edition. Copyright © 1992 by American Bible Society. Used by permission.

ISBN 1-57856-312-7

Copyright © 2001 by Brenda Poinsett

Library of Congress Cataloging-in-Publication Data

Poinsett, Brenda.
    Celebrations that touch the heart : creative ideas to make your holidays and special events meaningful / by Brenda Poinsett.— 1st ed.
        p. cm.
    Includes bibliographical references.
    ISBN 1-57856-312-7
      1. Holidays—United States—Planning. 2. Holidays—United States—Religious aspects.
    3. Special events—United States—Planning. 4. Special events—United States—Religious aspects. I. Title.

GT4803.A2 P65 2001
394.2`068—dc21
                                                 2001026265

Printed in the United States of America
2001—First Edition

10 9 8 7 6 5 4 3 2 1

To
Jim,
Joel,
and Ben,
for whom these ideas were collected
and with whom it is always a joy to celebrate.

CONTENTS

ACKNOWLEDGMENTS

I would like to thank the following people for ideas, inspiration, and encouragement. They helped me recognize and pursue my passion for celebrating with meaning.

My thanks go first of all to my mother, Lorene Spires, for planting within me the seeds of celebrating with meaning. Celebrations at her house are always filled with warmth and joy. The coffeepot is always on, and a freshly baked pie is ready to cut.

Thanks also go to Kay Forbes Dawson for sending us the pop-out nativity scene that sparked within me the determination to celebrate with meaning. She was helpful too with stories and resources for this book.

When my interest in celebrating with meaning began stirring, Kathy Hynson, Rose Bailey, Margaret Franklin, and Joyce Adams gave a workshop on keeping Christ in Christmas. I gleaned and gained from the ideas they presented then and through subsequent conversations with them, especially with Kathy.

Later when Pat Smith and I discovered that we share an interest in celebrating with meaning, we had the fun of giving many celebration workshops together. Judy Lancaster and Carileen Bollinger were also encouragers during this time.

Donna Williams also organized many workshops where I presented ideas and shared my enthusiasm. When Judy Bowman hosted a workshop, she encouraged me to put the ideas into a book, and Holly Kristan echoed her suggestion.

In working on the book, the following people read, critiqued, and edited the manuscript at various stages: Sherry Deirth, Pat McAlister, Sandy Emmett, Peggy Brooks, and my editor, Liz Heaney. Their help was invaluable in clarifying the ideas, and I am so grateful to them.

And, of course, I couldn't have written a book of this nature without the men in my life: my husband, Bob, and our sons, Jim, Joel, and Ben. I originally collected many of the ideas in this book for them, and I have been privileged to celebrate with them for many years. I look forward to more years of celebrations, which will now include a new family member: Joel's wife and our daughter-in-law, Eri.

Celebrating with meaning has added a richness to our family life that I wouldn't have wanted to miss. Thank you, readers, for letting me share these ideas with you.

CHAPTER 1

CELEBRATIONS THAT TOUCH THE HEART

Holidays come around year after year. As they arrive one by one, many of us do the same things over and over, rarely connecting our holiday activities with the meaning behind the day. This was true for my family until, quite by accident, I realized what we had been neglecting and missing.

When our sons, Jim and Joel, were four and a half and three, my husband and I moved away from family and friends so he could pursue graduate studies in another state. Our family of four settled into a tiny seven-hundred-square-foot house just in time for the fall semester to begin. We joined a church and began getting to know people. By Christmas, though, we had not made those vital connections that allow for warmth and closeness to occur naturally.

Bob was gone from home most of the time, spending hours studying in the library. So Jim, Joel, and I started to observe Christmas just like we always did. We shopped for gifts, but that didn't take long because we didn't have much money. We baked Christmas cookies, decorated a tree, and put up other decorations around the house. But we missed Bob, and we missed having friends stop by to see our tree and sample our cookies.

We had the trimmings of Christmas —decorations, a tree, gifts, food—but none of the season's warmth and richness. I told Bob, "It's like being all dressed up with nowhere to go."

I was still thinking about this when the mailman delivered a package from a friend back home marked, "Open Before

Christmas." With delight, the boys and I quickly opened the gift, a pop-out, cardboard nativity scene. Perhaps my friend suspected that we might need something to do. The boys and I immediately set to work popping out Mary, Joseph, baby Jesus, the shepherds, the Wise Men, the angel of the Lord, and the stable. While we assembled the pieces, I told the boys the story of Jesus' birth. Though I had read it to them before, I noticed an increased interest with this telling. The paper characters gave life to the story. When we finished, we arranged the pieces on the desk in the corner of our living room. I thought, *Well, that's the end of that. What a nice brief activity!*

I was wrong. To my surprise and delight, Jim and Joel kept playing with the figures the way they played with trucks in the sand pile. Sometimes I stopped what I was doing to listen to their reenactment of the drama. Other times they would run into the kitchen with a question or interrupt my writing with a comment. Each interruption gave me the opportunity to link Christmas with Jesus' birth, something I had always intended to do, but somehow hadn't gotten around to. We hadn't ignored the meaning of the holiday in earlier Christmases nor had we celebrated inappropriately, but we hadn't made a deliberate effort to focus on Jesus' birth and its significance. *Hmm*, I thought, *perhaps now is the time to get started.*

What We Gained

Focusing on meaning offered us spiritual activities we could do together, plus—and I hadn't expected this—it took away the loneliness of that particular Christmas and enriched the Christmases that followed. The results were so gratifying, I began to focus on the meaning of other holidays. Thanksgiving, Valentine's Day, St. Patrick's Day, especially Easter, and even Halloween lend themselves to celebrating various aspects of our faith. And the Fourth of July is an ideal time for emphasizing freedom— spiritual as well as political.

To celebrate with meaning is to know why, what, or who we are celebrating, so Bob and I usually had to educate our children about the holiday. We made the learning fun, treating it as part of the celebration.

Consequently, holidays at our home became vehicles for instruction and worship just as Passover, Pentecost, and the Feast of Tabernacles were for the ancient Israelites.

At Easter, for instance, we hid certain items inside plastic eggs to teach our children about Jesus' death and resurrection. One Easter Sunday morning, in a pinch for an activity for a Sunday school class of single adults, I grabbed the plastic eggs, put them in a basket, and took them to church. I passed around the basket in Sunday school and asked the adults to do what I always asked our sons to do: open the egg and explain the significance of the item inside. As the class did this, they touched thorns from my rosebush. They felt the coldness of a small metal cross and the sharpness of a nail's point. As I watched, I saw those adults respond in the same way Jim and Joel had when they played with the nativity scene. The adults connected with the event—God's historical work became real to them.

After that I was hooked. I deliberately

looked for opportunities to celebrate with meaning, not just with my family, but with Sunday school classes and other groups of people. I especially liked to emphasize meaning when we entertained guests in our home. The sights and sounds of each holiday provided a structure for sharing and celebrating our Christian faith and other important values. Now when we dressed up, we had great places to go!

THE CELEBRATION CIRCLE

To help my guests celebrate with meaning, I asked them to gather in a circle. Usually we sat around the dining table or made a circle of chairs in the family room. I wanted to include everyone, and this seating arrangement encouraged participation and closeness. In the middle of a holiday activity, I often noticed people smiling and radiating pleasure. I could tell they felt closer to each other and closer to God.

Although this warm sense of closeness didn't always happen, it happened enough that I wanted to experience it on other special days like birthdays, anniversaries, and significant occasions. On those days I wanted to affirm individuals, celebrate life, and recognize God's graciousness.

Would you like to have spiritual holidays, special moments, and meaningful celebrations? Would you like to grow closer to God and your loved ones? Would you like to show appreciation for others, affirming both who they are and what they mean to you? Would you like to express in creative ways your gratitude for your freedom, your heritage, and your very life?

Most of us do, but we hesitate because we think we can't do it or because we don't have time to plan meaningful activities or search for creative ideas. I understand. I had to work hard to discover fresh ideas that would work for my family or various groups. I often longed for a handbook where I could flip to the particular holiday or special occasion and find some creative and practical ideas. This book is the result of my efforts. It's a collection of simple, inexpensive, fun ideas that really work. Not meant to be read from beginning to end, *Celebrations That Touch the Heart* is a resource. Using the ideas presented here, even busy people will be able to celebrate with meaning.

Simple. Work requirements don't cease when it's time to celebrate. In fact, when I look at all that needs to be done at Christmastime, I understand why people leave their lights up all year round! With a few exceptions, the ideas in this book come with simple instructions and involve very little work. Small moments and little gestures can have a powerful impact. A simple sharing exercise at Thanksgiving, for instance, may be remembered far longer than the elegant meal that took hours to prepare.

Inexpensive. I can't even imagine what our family would have missed if we had put off celebrating until we had the money! Perhaps that's why I believe any family or group—no matter the income level, no matter what's in the bank account—should be able to celebrate with meaning. And with the ideas in this book, you can.

Fun. When we celebrate, I want everyone to have a good time. After our third child was born, I had to find creative ways to include him in our celebrations, given the age difference between him and his brothers. Ben didn't understand everything when he was small, but he could always enjoy being part of the celebration circle.

REDISCOVER THE JOY OF TRULY CELEBRATING

While there is a place for solemnity in celebration, for the most part *celebration* means fun and gaiety, something people need. When Mr. Tumnus described the awfulness of Narnia, he said, "Always winter and never Christmas, think of it!"[1] Winter without Christmas would be dismal indeed.

A life without celebrations would be dismal too. Whether your home contains one or two parents, whether you live close to relatives or far away, whether your family or group is large or small, rich or poor, you can celebrate with meaning. The simple, inexpensive, and fun activities in this book will show you how.

One more word. I've found that when we focus on meaning, our celebrations stay fresh and alive. We more freely express our feelings and our faith, and we can experience personal growth. We begin, for instance, to view freedom in a new light, gain a greater appreciation for a family member or friend, or to realize anew the significance of what God is doing in history and in our own lives. Celebrating with meaning also gives God a chance to work through us to bless our family and our friends. When we celebrate with meaning, our celebrations will truly touch the heart.

CHAPTER 2

EXPRESSING THE SENTIMENTS OF OUR HEARTS

Valentine's Day

Although Valentine's Day is a well-established American holiday, it's rather undefined. We celebrate it even though we're not exactly sure what we are celebrating. Maybe that's because the origin of Valentine's Day is shrouded in legends and myths.

We do know that pagan Romans had a feast in honor of Lupercus, a god whom they believed protected them from wolves. Once a year, in mid-February, people gathered to give thanks to Lupercus by feasting, dancing, and playing games. On the eve of this feast, young people held a celebration of their own, declaring their love for each other, proposing marriage, or choosing partners for the following year. (In the Roman republic, the new year started on March 1.)

As the Roman Empire became Christianized, many people stopped believing in Lupercus. However, the mid-February holiday was such a merry time that the Romans kept the traditional celebration. So, instead of honoring Lupercus, they honored Saint Valentine.

Valentine was a priest who lived in Rome during a time when Christians were persecuted. Some legends say that Valentine went to prison for his faith and that, when he refused to recant his belief in Christ, he was put to death. Another legend says that he was martyred for helping persecuted Christians. Some stories say he was beheaded for defying

VERSES WITH HEART

Thy word have I hid in mine heart, that I might not sin against thee.

Psalm 119:11

Trust in the LORD with all thine heart; and lean not unto thine own understanding. In all thy ways acknowledge him, and he shall direct thy paths.

Proverbs 3:5-6

For man looketh on the outward appearance, but the LORD looketh on the heart.

1 Samuel 16:7

For with the heart man believeth unto righteousness.

Romans 10:10

And thou shalt love the Lord thy God with all thy heart, and with all thy soul, and with all thy mind, and with all thy strength.

Mark 12:30

Search me, O God, and know my heart: try me, and know my thoughts.

Psalm 139:23

For as [a man] thinketh in his heart, so is he.

Proverbs 23:7

Delight thyself also in the LORD; and he shall give thee the desires of thine heart.

Psalm 37:4

Roman law and marrying young lovers. According to those accounts, the Roman emperor had ordered young men not to marry because he believed they would be more willing to go to war if they did not have wives. Moved by compassion for the young lovers, Valentine married them secretly.

This confusion about Saint Valentine might be clarified by the theory that there were two priests named Valentine during this time in history. At least one of them was martyred on February 14, A.D. 270, the day before the old Roman celebration. When Christianity became the official religion of Rome, the church merged the Roman holiday with the martyrdom of Saint Valentine on February 14.

Through the years "Saint" was dropped from the holiday's name, making it simply "Valentine's Day" with the focus on celebrating love. Although the day is often linked with romantic love, it is also a natural time for recognizing other kinds of love. As Phyllis Stanley and Miltinnie Yih say in their book *Celebrate the Seasons,* "Valentine's Day is a time for hearts and flowers, friendship and love. It is a day for expressing love and affection in prose and poetry, for seeking to communicate the sentiments of our hearts."[1]

Clearly, Valentine's Day offers a wide range of possibilities for celebration. My three sons, for instance, weren't interested in sending valentine cards to each person in their classes at school ("Yuck, do we *have* to?"). As they brought home their required artwork, I thought, *Surely we can find a spiritual emphasis amid the cupids, flowers, hearts, and doilies.* The first thing that popped into my mind was the Bible verse "Thy word have I hid in mine heart, that I might not sin against

[God]" (Psalm 119:11). *Why not hide God's word in our hearts during this season of hearts?* And that is what we have done, year after year.

You might find that this idea works for your family. Or you might want to try to learn more about Saint Valentine and talk about him at dinner on Valentine's Day. Or you could focus on expressing your love and appreciation for certain people in your life. It's up to you. What are the sentiments of your heart? And how do you want to express them?

FILL YOUR HEART WITH GOD'S WORD

To give a holiday touch to our February scripture memory activity, I made three mailboxes. Our sons liked placing mail in our rural mailbox, putting up the flag, and looking for return mail. So I printed Bible verses on the back of valentines—the ones leftover from the packets bought for their classmates! When they had memorized the verses on the back of their valentines, they quoted them to my husband. For every verse they memorized, Bob gave our boys a stamp (a valentine sticker). Then each boy put the valentine in an envelope, stamped it, put it in the mailbox, and put up the flag. Early the next morning, the mailman (me) came in tooth-fairy fashion, took their letters, and left a reward (a piece of gum, a quarter, or a snack-size candy bar) for each verse memorized. Our sons didn't get an allowance and seldom had candy, so these rewards were both an incentive and a celebration. After leaving the treat, I put the flag back down so the boys would be ready for another day of hiding God's Word in their hearts.

A SIMPLE CRAFT

To make replicas of rural mailboxes, use long rectangular boxes with an opening at one end. Cover each box with several sheets of white tissue paper or with construction paper. Print the child's name on the side of the box. Cut a long, narrow piece of cardboard for the arm of the flag. At one end of the arm, glue a red heart for the flag. Attach the opposite end of the arm to the box with a brad. (A brad is like a metallic tack, but instead of a point, it has two arms that fan out after it has been inserted. It will hold the flag to the box and yet allow the flag to move up and down.) Now you're ready for your valentine memory work!

We enjoyed this activity for many years. When the boys were small, I gave them short verses containing the word *heart*. After they memorized those, we moved on to more general verses, and that's when I included the verse that is a favorite of parents everywhere: "Children, obey your parents in the Lord, for this is right" (Ephesians 6:1, NIV).

As our sons grew older, they memorized longer passages of Scripture: the Love Chapter (1 Corinthians 13), the Lord's Prayer, the books of the Bible, and the Ten Commandments (Exodus 20). All five of us looked forward to this activity every year. (Bob and I found the boys' memorization efforts sharpening our own Scripture memory!) February was set aside for Scripture memory work—and those efforts were a fun and significant way to celebrate Valentine's Day.

FILL YOUR HEART WITH LOVE

Valentine's Day can also call for a special meal. One woman couldn't afford a romantic meal out with her husband, so she decided to have a romantic dinner for their whole family. She cut out heart-shaped confetti from red and pink construction paper, created a special valentine for each family member, and decorated the table with Hershey's Kisses and ribbon curls. She brought out her good china, crystal goblets, and candles to set the mood. She even served the food in heart-shaped dishes and baked a heart-shaped chocolate cake for dessert.[2]

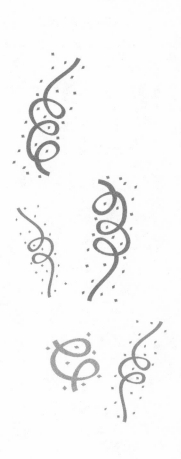

Her family loved it, and so will yours, but don't stop with the décor! Be sure to use this occasion to point to the Lord's love:

- Before saying the blessing or between the main course and dessert, ask someone to read 1 Corinthians 13:4-7, where the apostle Paul defines love. Read from a modern translation such as *The Living Bible* or *The Message*.

- Prepare printed copies of 1 Corinthians 13:4-7 for everyone to read either together or responsively.

VALENTINE PARTY IDEAS

Here are some ideas for a Valentine's party full of fun and laughter, one that creates a warm atmosphere just right for talking about love.

- Build around a red and white theme. Ask everyone to come dressed in red and white, bring a red or white dessert, and be prepared to tell what makes them blush. During the first few minutes of the party, ask each guest to find out from at least three other people what things would be most likely to make them blush or pale—turn red or white.[3]

- Make up limericks for each of your guests and let them fill in the last line. A limerick is a five-line poem in which the first two lines and the last line rhyme. The third and fourth lines are much shorter, and they also rhyme. As an example, imagine a Barry and Carrie among your guests. You could write:

    There was a young lady named Carrie
    Who's sweet on a fellow name Barry
    It's easy to know
    That wherever they go
    (guests fill in last line).

- Buy some of those candy conversation hearts that have two- or three-word sayings on them: "I love you," "Lover Boy," "Turtle Dove," "Kiss Me," and so on. One guest should

(continued on p. 13)

- Ahead of time, ask family members to write their own paraphrases of 1 Corinthians 13 and then share their thoughts at the table. You might ask younger children to draw a picture showing some aspect of love mentioned in this passage. They could also make a rebus of one verse of the passage. To do this, print a verse on a large piece of paper and leave blank spaces for some of the nouns. Then have children look in magazines for pictures to represent the nouns and paste them in the spaces.

- Ask the adults and older children to bring something that reminds them of love—a letter, a gift, a song, a book, or a poem—and have them present their items to the group, telling why it reminds them of love.

Use Hearts to Express Your Sentiments

As you celebrate this holiday, let the red hearts remind you to celebrate love—your love for those close to you, your love for God, and his love for you.

- Make fourteen red hearts from construction paper. Each one should be about 3 x 3.5 inches. Number the hearts from one to fourteen and place the pile of hearts in the center of your dining table, which you've covered with a white tablecloth. The number one should be on top. Before the meal begins, ask family members and/or guests to pick up a heart, one person at a time, and tell why he or she loves God. Don't take turns. Just let participants spontaneously reach for a heart as they think of reasons why they love God. (Using fourteen hearts ties in with the holiday—February 14—and also lets guests know this activity will be brief. They will be more comfortable participating when they know how long it will last.)

- A week before Valentine's Day, place some plain red and pink construction-paper hearts, some felt-tip pens, and a small basket on a table in a convenient location. Ask family members to take the time before February 14 to write on the hearts why they love God and then put the hearts in the basket. At your main meal on Valentine's Day, bring the basket to the table, which you have covered with a white tablecloth. Scatter the hearts around the table. Ask participants to pick up the hearts near them and read aloud what is written on them. In your prayer before the meal say something like this: "Father, our hearts are full of love for you." (This idea can also be used for focusing on family love. Ask family members to write on the hearts why they love their family. At the table, read aloud what is written and say, "See how much we love each other.")

- If you have small children, write out on red and pink construction-paper hearts Bible verses that speak of God's love for us. Hide these hearts around the house as if they were Easter eggs. Invite the children to search for the hearts and to

pick one of the candies from a bowl and, following the regular rules for charades, try to pantomime the message.[4]

- As each guest arrives, pin the name of one member of a famous couple on his/her back. Guests must first learn the name on their back by asking other guests yes and no questions and then find their "mate," who becomes their dinner partner. Some famous couples you might include are Abraham and Sarah, Adam and Eve, Samson and Delilah, and Romeo and Juliet.

- Poetry is a February 14 tradition. Borrow the "Roses are red, Violets are blue" rhyme and ask guests to rewrite the last two lines, or encourage them to make up their own poems. You might also have a poetry reading and ask each guest to bring a favorite love poem.

- Add to the collection of tales and legends about the origin of Valentine's Day. Ask guests to make up their own original story about how and why Valentine's Day began. Perhaps your story would be about a prince who won the heart of his princess and, as they rode out of sight, shouted, "Happy V Day to all and to all a Good Heart."[5]

We love him, because he first loved us.

clap when they find one. Read the verses aloud. If your kids are older, you might just scatter the hearts around on the table or place one at each person's plate. Have each person read what's on their paper heart before saying the blessing.

EXPRESSING OUR LOVE FOR OTHERS

- *Valentine compliments.* Cut out a small construction-paper heart for everyone present and print their names on the hearts. Place the hearts in a basket. With everyone seated in a circle, ask each to draw a heart from the basket. Let each person, one by one, read the name drawn and then say one thing that he/she loves about that person. For example, "Sandra, the love of the Lord is so obvious in you. He loves us all through you!" or "Sandra, you always amaze me by how many of the details you remember about my life. You are so sensitive and caring." If you have time, ask everyone in the circle to say something nice about the person whose name was read. Continue around the circle until each person has received his or her valentine compliments.

- *Heart of Love mural.* Give each child a 6-inch square of white construction paper and crayons or felt-tip markers. Ask them to draw pictures of people they love. Cut an extra-large heart out of red paper. Write the words "We love you" in the center of the heart. Help the children glue their pictures to the red heart. When the glue has dried, hang the heart on a dining room wall so it can prompt table talk about whom we love and why.

- *Handmade Candygrams.* For a Valentine's Day treat, write each of your children a love letter on poster board using strategically placed packages of their favorite candies to help convey your message. You might, for example, use a box of Junior Mints to say, "We were 'mint' to be together."

VERSES THAT SPEAK OF GOD'S LOVE

For God so loved the world, that he gave his only begotten Son, that whosoever believeth in him should not perish, but have everlasting life.

John 3:16

Yea, I have loved thee with an everlasting love: therefore with lovingkindness have I drawn thee.

Jeremiah 31:3

God commendeth his love toward us, in that, while we were yet sinners, Christ died for us.

Romans 5:8

Behold, what manner of love the Father hath bestowed upon us, that we should be called the sons of God.

1 John 3:1

Herein is love, not that we loved God, but that he loved us, and sent his Son to be the propitiation for our sins.

1 John 4:10

We love him, because he first loved us.

1 John 4:19

"I LOVE YOU BECAUSE..."

Debbie Fick didn't just write a note of love. She wrote books of love for her children. She writes, "I bought four different blank books and wrote a personal letter to each child in the front of each book, telling them how and why I loved them. I included all my hopes and dreams for them, as well as an individual prayer. After pouring out my heart about my love, goals, and desires for them, I included all their spiritual milestones (names, dates, times, and celebrations). I shared meaningful Scripture passages that touched my heart, or words to special songs—and why they were important to me. I included their own comments about the things they'd achieved toward their own goals, as well. The contents of each book were individualized for each child, making each a very unique and special gift.

"One of the most enjoyable parts of making these books was the scavenger hunt I organized for them after school on Valentine's Day in order to surprise them with the books. Awaiting them in their rooms at the end of the hunt were a heart-shaped box of candy and the beautifully wrapped gift of my 'I love you because' book. It's something I hope they'll always cherish, even if life leads us in different directions."[6]

- *A hunt that ends in love.* Celebrate your love and affection for your children by hiding small, inexpensive gifts throughout the house. Help them find their gifts by offering a series of rhyming clues. For example, using the clue "If you want a treat to eat, don't sit on your seat. Instead go to where you hear the beat!" you might hide near the stereo some candy hearts with words of love written on them. Let your last clue lead to a letter you have written or a card you have purchased that expresses your love for your child.

EXPRESS YOUR SENTIMENTS WITH CARDS

Legend has it that when Valentine was jailed for helping Christians, he cured his jailer's daughter of blindness. Some also say he fell in love with the girl and wrote her love notes. Before he died, he wrote a final note to her and signed it "From your Valentine." As Valentine apparently knew, written notes can powerfully express our sentiments. Greeting cards can too. So work together as a family or group and make your own valentines to tell others how you feel and that you care about them.

1. Make and take valentines to lonely and/or elderly people.

2. Send valentines to people whose mates have died in the past year.

3. Write love notes and tuck them in your family's lunch boxes, notebooks, or briefcases.

4. Make valentines in which you say why you thank God for this person.

5. Write a note of appreciation to someone in the community or the church, someone like the nursery coordinator or the custodian, whose work regularly goes unrecognized.

Before we knew what the heart was actually shaped like, we thought it looked like the heart we see on valentines and that it was the center of our feelings. We know now that the brain is the center, but we still use old heart sayings to indicate our feelings. For example, have you ever said "He broke my heart" or "It does my heart good to hear you say that"?

Valentine's Day, with its traditions of cupids, red roses, and heart-shaped boxes of candy, is often linked with romance, but its heart symbol makes it a natural for emphasizing love. Let red hearts remind you to celebrate love—your love for family and friends, your love for God, and his love for us.

How about designing a card for an elderly person who never forgets to send your children birthday cards?

> Roses are red.
> Praises to the sky.
> My children love you,
> And so do I.[7]

CHAPTER 3

SOMEONE EVERYONE OUGHT TO KNOW

Saint Patrick's Day

Americans—Irish or not—have long embraced Saint Patrick's Day as a holiday, but most know little about the saint for whom the day is named. Patrick was born into a prominent and wealthy family somewhere in pre–Anglo Saxon Britain between A.D. 385 and 389. When he was nearly sixteen, Irish raiders captured him along with many others, took them to Ireland, and sold them as slaves.

As a slave, Patrick cared for his master's sheep. Life was hard, unlike anything he had experienced at home in Britain. Many times, while enduring cold, long rains and harsh winds, he had to stay up for days and nights on end to protect his flock from wolves or robbers.[1] But these hardships deepened Patrick's faith in God. Before his abduction, he seldom prayed, but while tending sheep, he prayed frequently. Patrick's faith increased, and he sensed God at work in his captivity.

After six years of slavery, Patrick finally escaped. Traveling the back roads and hiding much of the time, he made his way about two hundred miles to the sea and took a ship back home. When he arrived, Patrick's family welcomed him with all the pomp and ceremony due a returning nobleman. Installed once again in his ancestral estates and given his father's seat in the legislature, Patrick may never have intended to leave his native land again, but God had other plans.

BOAT SALADS

Our sons loved the boat salads I often served at our home for Saint Patrick's Days. I made an individual salad for each child. As they ate, I would tell the story of Patrick's escape from slavery.

To make a boat salad, you will need green Jell-O, canned Bartlett pear halves, straws, and small triangular flags made out of construction paper. Prepare the Jell-O according to package directions. When the Jell-O has reached a soft set, scoop it onto individual salad plates. The softness of the Jell-O gives the impression of water. Then place a pear half with the rounded side up on the bed of Jell-O. Slit one-third of each straw. In the slit, insert a flag. Stick the other end of the straw in the pear, and you have a boat sailing on the green sea.

Before long Patrick had a vision, and he became deeply convinced that he must return to Ireland, which was largely pagan. After many setbacks and several years of religious study, he finally did return to the land where he had been enslaved. Immersed in magic and superstition, the Irish severely opposed Patrick, who preached from the Scriptures with persuasive eloquence. According to one account, "With great faithfulness [Patrick] shared Scripture and the teaching of the Christian faith, converting chieftains and their clans, winning the pagan population to Christ, baptizing new believers, planting churches, and training leaders for those churches. When Patrick died on March 17, around A.D. 461, the church was firmly established in Ireland."[2] Saint Patrick's Day commemorates the anniversary of his death.

THE STORY BEHIND THE HOLIDAY

- Tell Saint Patrick's story at your family's main meal on March 17 or at a Saint Patrick's Day party. Serve something green in honor of the occasion. Broccoli or Brussels sprouts may not excite your children, but they will like green Jell-O, pistachio pudding, green pancakes (add green food coloring to your regular batter), or sugar cookies with green icing. Better yet, put two or three drops of green food coloring in clear glasses. Don't let anyone see you. When the children come to the table, pour milk into the glasses. When the milk swirls green, you'll definitely get their attention!

- Add a dramatic flair to the story by asking a friend or family member to dress as Saint Patrick and tell his story in the first person ("When I was sixteen, I was taken prisoner…"). A portrait of Patrick in the Hugh Lane Municipal Gallery of Modern Art in Dublin shows him wearing a long flowing white garment similar to what a priest might wear. Around Patrick's waist is a belt, and a long cloak hangs from his shoulders. He's bearded, wears sandals, and carries a crooked staff.

- Saint Patrick's life had many interesting twists and turns. If you think your children would find it hard to sit still through the whole story, you may want to focus on only a few parts. For example, you can tell how Patrick escaped from slavery and how God protected him and provided him with passage on a ship so he could return home. Here are some scenes to share:

  - After serving six years as a slave, Patrick heard a voice in his sleep saying to him, "Thou fastest well and you soon will return to your country." After a little while, he heard the message, "Look, a ship is ready for you." Somehow Patrick managed to get away and find his way to the seacoast (a trip of two hundred miles) where, in fact, a ship was ready to leave port.[3]

RECOMMENDED READING

Need to review the details of Saint Patrick's story? Here are two good sources.

- Chapter 2 of *Men Who Made Missions* by historian Leon McBeth. This is a nonfiction book for adult readers.

- *Tales of Saint Patrick* by Eileen Dunlap. Written for eight to twelve year olds, this is an absorbing fictionalized account of Saint Patrick's life based on Patrick's own writings and other ancient sources.

MAKE YOUR OWN SHAMROCK CENTERPIECE

Have your children cut out at least twenty shamrocks (all the same size) from green construction paper. Use tape to attach a shamrock to one end of a tongue depressor, a kabobs spear, or some other long flat stick. Glue another shamrock on the back of the first one. Set the shamrock wands aside to dry. Put them in a vase to use as your centerpiece for Saint Patrick's Day dinner.

■ When Patrick arrived, the ship was preparing to sail. When he asked for passage, the captain turned him down. He was not interested in giving passage to a ragged and penniless youth. Just then several Irish wolfhounds were brought aboard, snarling and snapping at their terrified trainer. Patrick, who had worked with such dogs like this, spoke to them in Gaelic, the language they knew. His voice soothed and calmed them, and the captain was so impressed that he changed his mind. He told Patrick he could earn his fare by taking care of the wolfhounds.[4]

HANG A CROSS ON THE DOOR

As a family, make a small wooden cross and hang it on your front door to remind yourselves of the courage of Patrick and the Christians who helped him escape from slavery and make his way to the coast. While there is little information about Patrick's escape, historian Leon McBeth believes that Christians marked their humble cabins with a small wooden cross so Patrick would know where to stop. "In 'underground railroad' fashion, they passed him from one Christian family to another until he came at last to the sea."[5]

THE THREE IN ONE, THE ONE IN THREE

We associate the color green with Ireland because of the lush green color of the land. Vegetation grows well in the mild, moist climate, and shamrock clover grows everywhere. As legend tells it, Patrick

often used a shamrock leaf to illustrate the Trinity. While this teaching method can't be verified, his writings do reveal his strong belief in the Trinity, and a shamrock leaf with its three parts is an effective visual reminder of the interrelationship of the Father, the Son, and the Holy Spirit.

In March most supermarkets sell pots of shamrocks. Purchase one to use as your centerpiece on Saint Patrick's Day. Sometime during

THE BREASTPLATE

I arise today through
  God's strength to pilot me:
God's might to uphold me,
God's wisdom to guide me,
God's eye to look before me,
God's ear to hear me,
God's word to speak for me,
God's hand to guard me,
God's way to lie before me,
God's shield to protect me.

Christ with me, Christ before me,
  Christ behind me,
Christ in me, Christ beneath me,
  Christ above me,
Christ on my right, Christ on my left,
Christ when I lie down,
Christ when I sit down,
Christ when I arise,
Christ in the heart of every man
  who thinks of me,
Christ in the mouth of everyone
  who speaks of me,
Christ in every eye that sees me,
Christ in every ear that hears me.[7]

dinner, call attention to the centerpiece and explain how the leaf is one yet three. If you note this connection between the shamrock and the Trinity before you eat, use the last lines of the hymn "Come, Thou Almighty King" as your family's prayer.

> To Thee, great One in Three,
>
> Eternal praises be,
>
> Hence evermore;
>
> His sov'reign majesty
>
> May we in glory see,
>
> And to eternity
>
> Love and adore.[6]

CELEBRATE WITH PRAYER

• Patrick fervently believed he was commissioned by the Lord to preach the gospel to every creature (Mark 16:15). In obedience, he returned to Ireland and converted much of that country to Christianity during his lifetime. This achievement ranks among the outstanding missionary feats of Christian history. Long after he died, his disciples continued his work. Patrick's fervency and devotion can remind us to celebrate the work of today's missionaries. At your family's main meal on Saint Patrick's Day, offer thanks and prayers for missionaries you know and for the important work they are doing.

- Patrick was a man of prayer. From the time of his conversion as a young man until his last days, he made prayer an integral part of his life. His writings tell how he prayed hundreds of prayers, day and night, in all kinds of conditions and various situations. Many people believe that he wrote a prayer called "The Breastplate." You may want to print copies of it from this book and pray it together as a group.

Wouldn't you like Saint Patrick's Day to be more than an excuse to wear green and eat corned beef and cabbage? Why not let the day become a celebration of the Trinity, an opportunity to learn more about a great missionary, and a time to pray for missionaries who presently serve the Lord?

THE TRINITY IN OUR EXPERIENCE

The grace of the Lord Jesus Christ, and the love of God, and the communion of the Holy Ghost, be with you all.

2 Corinthians 13:14

CHAPTER 4

THE CROSS AND THE RESURRECTION

Easter

At Easter we celebrate the hallmarks of our Christian faith: Jesus' saving death on the cross, which provided forgiveness for our sins and acceptance into God's family (Romans 5:8; 1 John 3:1), and his Resurrection, which assures us of victory over sin and death as well as eternal life with God (1 Corinthians 15:55-57; John 3:16). These events, rich in meaning and drama, make for glorious celebration and worship in our Holy Week and Easter Sunday church services.

But on the home front, I found it challenging to celebrate Easter. The Christmas story is wonderful. A baby is born, and he will be the King of kings and Lord of lords, bringing joy, peace, and love to the world. No unpalatable details here! But Easter... How could I help my family celebrate something as profound and mysterious as the Resurrection? It's impossible to get to the joyful, wonder-filled part of the story without first walking through some ugly, very sobering events—betrayal, injustice, sorrow, death, and pain—yet I wanted my children to appreciate Jesus' sacrifice.

I was thinking about how to do this when I saw a small article in the magazine *Evangelizing Today's Child*. I read about how a teacher used plastic Easter eggs to quiz her students about the details of Jesus' crucifixion. After putting symbols of the story inside the eggs, she passed them out and asked each student to open an egg, identify what was in it, and talk about how it connects with the Easter story. *Aha,* I thought, *I can use that idea with our family.*

My husband and I brainstormed our own list of items that could represent elements of the Easter story. We gathered the items and put each one in a brightly colored plastic egg. On the Wednesday before Easter, I put a basket with five eggs in it on the middle of our dining table. At dinner each family member selected an egg from the basket, opened it, and explained what the item inside had to do with the Easter story. We did this each day as the week progressed, adding more eggs with new items each day. As we touched thorns, the leather of a scourging whip, and a hard stone, our family gained a new appreciation of what Jesus did for us.

I lost that issue of *Evangelizing Today's Child* long ago, but we haven't lost the activity. It holds the record for the longest-running tradition at our home. Our two oldest sons were preschoolers when we started doing this. Today all three of our sons are adults, yet we still celebrate Easter this way when they come home. If we have guests, they get to open an egg too. I've also used this activity many times with Sunday school classes.

The Easter Story in Eggshells

Here is a list of the items we included in our eggs, a brief explanation of their significance, and biblical references to them.

- *A small plastic donkey.* Jesus made his triumphal entry into Jerusalem on a donkey (Matthew 21:1-9; Mark 11:1-10; Luke 19:29-38; John 12:12-15, NIV).

- *Plastic leaves resembling palm leaves.* The cheering crowd spread palm leaves before Jesus when he entered Jerusalem (Matthew 21:1-9; Mark 11:1-10; John 12:12-13).

- *Tiny bottle of perfume.* A woman lovingly poured out expensive perfume on Jesus, anointing him for burial (Matthew 26:6-13; Mark 14:3-9; John 12:1-8).

- *A dime.* Judas received thirty pieces of silver for delivering Jesus over to his enemies (Matthew 26:14-16; Luke 22:3-6).

- *A small plastic lamb.* Jesus celebrated the Feast of Unleavened Bread with his disciples. It was the day the lambs for the Passover were killed (Mark 14:12; Luke 22:7-8,14-16). Jesus became the sacrificial Lamb for our sins.

- *A small piece of bread.* When Jesus and his disciples ate the Last Supper, Jesus explained that the bread he broke symbolized his body (Matthew 26:26-30; Mark 14:22-26; Luke 22:19-20).

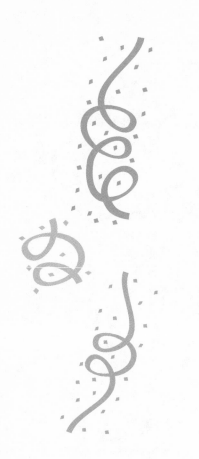

- *Some plastic grapes.* The wine the disciples and Jesus drank at the Last Supper symbolized Jesus' blood (Matthew 26:26-30; Mark 14:22-26; Luke 22:17-20).

- *Small plastic rooster.* Jesus predicted that Peter would deny him three times before the rooster crowed (Matthew 26:31-35, 69-75; Mark 14:27-31,66-72; Luke 22:31-34,54-62; John 13:36-38; 18:15-18,25-27).

- *Plastic toothpick shaped like a sword.* Peter used a sword to cut off the ear of one of the men who came to arrest Jesus (Matthew 26:47-56; Mark 14:43-50; Luke 22:47-53; John 18:3-11), and a soldier plunged a sword into Jesus' side as he hung on the cross (John 19:31-37).

- *A chain.* Roman soldiers bound Jesus and led him to appear before Pilate, the Roman governor (Matthew 27:1-2; Mark 15:1).

- *Leather shoestring* with sharp pieces of metal tied in the ends. Jesus was scourged with a whip that had sharp bits of metal in the ends (Mark 15:19; John 19:1).

- *Thorns from a rosebush.* Pilate's soldiers made a crown of thorns and placed it on Jesus' head (Matthew 27:29; Mark 15:17; John 19:2,5).

- *Purple piece of cloth.* In mockery Roman soldiers put a purple robe on Jesus (Mark 15:17; John 19:2-5).

- *Small metal cross.* Jesus was crucified on a cross (Matthew 27:31-35; Mark 15:20-22; Luke 23:26,32-33; John 19:17; Philippians 2:8).

- *A pair of dice.* At the foot of the cross, the Roman soldiers gambled for Jesus' clothes (Matthew 27:35; Mark 15:24; Luke 23:34; John 19:23-24).

- *Small sponge.* As he hung on the cross, Jesus said he was thirsty, and someone lifted up a sponge soaked with cheap wine (Matthew 27:48; Mark 15:36; John 19:28-30).

- *Small piece of linen cloth.* Joseph of Arimathea wrapped Jesus' body in linen (Matthew 27:59; Mark 15:46; Luke 23:53; John 19:40, 20:4-7).

- *Rock.* A stone was placed in front of the tomb (Matthew 27:60; Mark 15:46, 16:3-4), and an angel of the Lord later rolled it away (Matthew 28:2).

- *Whole cloves.* Faithful women took spices to the tomb to anoint Jesus' body (Mark 16:1), and Nicodemus and Joseph used spices to prepare his body for burial (John 19:39-41).

A SIMPLE CENTERPIECE

On Resurrection Sunday place a single, empty plastic egg in a basket of Easter grass in the center of your table. Before the blessing, ask a family member to open the egg. Ask, "What does the empty egg stand for?" When someone says, "The empty tomb," reply, "He is risen!" Have someone else at the table ready to respond with the other part of this traditional Easter greeting: "He is risen indeed!"

- *Nail.* When Jesus was crucified, soldiers drove nails into his hands (John 20:24-25).

NOT EGGS-ACTLY ALIKE

Many families have used memento-filled eggs to celebrate Jesus' death and resurrection. From them I've gleaned some ideas that might work for you.

- Put the corresponding Bible verses in the eggs with the items. This is particularly helpful if family members are not familiar with the events of the days immediately preceding and following Jesus' crucifixion. Another option is to have a modern translation of the Bible at the table. When an egg is opened, read the Bible verse (or verses) that refer to the item. Later in the week or in another Easter season, use the eggs to prompt a retelling of Jesus' death and resurrection.

- Select twelve items to go into twelve eggs and place them in an egg carton. Number the eggs to match the order of the items as they appear in the story. Each evening at bedtime during Easter week, tell the biblical account of Jesus' death and resurrection, opening each egg to display its contents at the appropriate time in the story.

- Plan to read together the Bible's account of Jesus' death and resurrection during Holy Week. Select a portion of Scripture to read each day. After the day's reading, ask family members to identify what objects could remind them of what was read. Assign family members to collect the items and bring them the next time you gather to read the Easter story. At that time, review what each item symbolizes. Then read a new portion of Scripture and again ask family members to identify and collect key objects. Keep all the gathered items in a large basket. Use the filled basket as your centerpiece for Easter Sunday meals.

DECORATE EGGS WITH CHRISTIAN SYMBOLS

Our culture recognizes eggs as a symbol of spring, a sign of new life. But we can see in them greater meaning. We can let Easter eggs represent the new life and hope of Jesus' resurrection. Celebrate this by decorating dyed eggs with Christian symbols.

You can dye either hard-boiled or blown eggs, depending on how long you want to keep your creations. For blown eggs, carefully prick a hole at each end of an eggshell and blow out the inside of the egg. Let the eggshells dry out overnight before dying them.

Dye won't stick where you have drawn with wax or a crayon so, using a white crayon or clear wax, put the following symbols on your eggs:

- different styles of crosses

- a crown of thorns

SQUEEZED FOR TIME?

If you don't have time to prepare your own set of Easter eggs and items, you may want to purchase Resurrection Eggs at a local Christian bookstore. The kit offers twelve eggs packaged in an egg carton, each one containing a symbol of Holy Week. Also included are twelve brief child-friendly lessons. You can use these Resurrection Eggs for brief hands-on devotionals on the twelve days leading up to Easter or as a one-time activity on Easter Sunday.

- a triangle, representing the Trinity

- the Christian fish, the secret sign of early believers

- a circle, representing everlasting life

And what can you do with all of your eggs when you have finished decorating them?

- Put them in a bowl or basket for your Easter centerpiece.

- Give them as a gift.

- Hang blown eggs on an Easter-egg tree. To make an Easter-egg tree, find a nice dry branch and spray paint it white or yellow—any spring color you like. Anchor it in a bowl or basket with clay, a Styrofoam block, or something heavy enough to keep it from tipping over. Glue ribbons to your eggs and hang them on the tree. The symbols on the eggs make good conversation starters when you have guests in your home.

PALM SUNDAY

Hang a large piece of newsprint on the wall near your dining table. Cut a large donkey out of brown construction paper. Place it on one end of the newsprint. In front of the donkey, draw a path. Then, on

Saturday night before Palm Sunday (perhaps at dinner), tell how the people praised Jesus as he rode the donkey into Jerusalem (Matthew 21:1-11; Mark 11:1-10; John 12:12-19).

Cut several large palm leaves out of green construction paper, and have them ready on Sunday morning. At breakfast, ask each person to write words of praise on one side of a palm leaf. On the other side have them write something they need to repent of. Glue the palm leaves along the path (praise side up!), just as they were laid on Jesus' path when he entered Jerusalem (Matthew 21:8; Mark 11:8).[1] Repentance cleanses us, making room for genuine praise in our hearts, and repentance can be done privately as well as publicly. Turning our sins toward the wall reminds us that God does not remember our sin and count it against us (Isaiah 43:25; Psalm 103:12).

A Thursday Night Reflection

Easter isn't about a bunny; it's about a sacrificed lamb. Each year Jews celebrate the Feast of Passover to commemorate the escape of God's people from Egyptian slavery. Passover is a remembrance of how God instructed the Jews to sacrifice a lamb and smear its blood on the doorposts of their homes so that the Lord would spare the life of the oldest son in that household. The blood of the lamb caused the Lord to "pass over" the homes of the Israelites. Since the doorposts of Egyptian homes had no blood on them, Egyptian families lost their oldest son. In the aftermath of this tragedy, Pharaoh allowed Moses to lead the Jews out of Egypt.

RECOMMENDED READING

On the Saturday night before Palm Sunday, start reading C. S. Lewis's *The Lion, the Witch, and the Wardrobe* with your children. In seventeen short chapters, this book tells the story of how Aslan, a noble lion symbolic of Jesus, frees Narnia from the spell of the White Witch. Aslan dies in the process and comes back to life. It's a great story that will help children, teens, and adults appreciate and perhaps even better understand the death and resurrection of Jesus Christ.

THE PASSOVER-EASTER CONNECTION

The death and resurrection of Jesus occurred at the time of the Jewish Passover. In the early years of Christianity, Jewish Christians observed the Resurrection and Passover together on the fourteenth day of Nisan, the Jewish month roughly corresponding to April. However, Gentile Christians celebrated the Resurrection every Sunday with a special emphasis on the Sunday closest to Nisan 14. To settle this difference, churchmen at the Nicene Council in A.D. 325 fixed the date of Easter on the first Sunday following the Paschal full moon. That is the first full moon after the vernal equinox, March 21. This system is still followed today. Therefore, Easter Sunday moves between March 22 and April 25.

Jesus is called the "Lamb of God" because he gave himself as a Passover sacrifice for our sins. His shed blood allows us to escape the eternal death penalty for our sins.

Jesus celebrated the Passover meal with his disciples on Thursday night before his death. You might want to recreate this meal and imagine what it would have been like to be among the disciples that evening. *Celebrate the Feasts* by Martha G. Zimmerman contains directions, recipes, and an entire worship service. Instructions minus the recipes are also available in *Parties with a Purpose* by Marlene LeFever. Check with your public or church library for more resources.

When Jesus shared that last Passover meal with his disciples, he instituted a new celebration feast. He took bread, gave thanks, broke it, and gave it to them saying, "This is my body, which is for you. Do this in memory of me" (1 Corinthians 11:24, TEV). In the same way, he took the cup of wine saying, "This cup is God's new covenant, sealed with my blood. Whenever you drink it, do so in memory of me" (1 Corinthians 11:25, TEV).

On the Thursday before Easter, have your own memorial supper of bread and wine (or grape juice) in remembrance of Jesus' death or attend a communion service.

FRIDAY, THE DARK DAY

On Friday afternoon Jesus was mocked, beaten, and executed on a cross. His followers were confused and despairing. This blackest of times deserves serious reflection. Here are some ways to encourage reflection:

- As a family, make three crosses from twigs, limbs, or craft sticks. Discuss the sadness of the day when Jesus was killed. Hang the crosses by your front door. You might even drape them with black.

- Light three candles to symbolize the three crosses on Calvary, the three times Peter denied Jesus that day, and the three days Jesus lay in the tomb. Talk about the Crucifixion and pray that God will help you understand the price Jesus paid for your sins. Dramatize the blackness of death at the end of the evening by turning out all the house lights and then blow out the candles.[2]

- Serve hot cross buns as a reminder of the Cross and the Resurrection. The cross of icing reminds us of Jesus' death, and the yeast in the rolls is a sign of new life. Yeast appears to have no life in it, yet when it is combined with other ingredients it causes dough to rise. Likewise, when Jesus is in our lives, he raises us to new life. (You will find hot cross buns in many supermarkets and bakeries near Easter. Or if you want to make your own, consult major cookbooks such as *Betty Crocker's Cookbook* and *The Fannie Farmer Cookbook*.)

THE LEGEND OF THE DOGWOOD

The dogwood was once the size of an oak tree, and because it was so firm and strong, it was chosen as the timber for the cross. To be used for such a cruel purpose greatly distressed the tree. In his gentle pity for all sorrow and suffering, Jesus said to the dogwood tree, "Because of your regret and pity for my suffering, never again shall the dogwood tree grow large enough to be used as a cross. Henceforth it shall be slender and bent and twisted and its blossoms shall be in the form of a cross—two long and two short petals. And in the center of the outer edge of each petal there will be nail prints, brown with rust and stained with red, and in the center of the flower will be a crown of thorns, and all who see it will remember."

• If dogwoods are in bloom where you live, bring some in for a centerpiece. Share with your family the legend of the dogwood as a way to focus on the cross.

SOMBER SATURDAY

Tell or review the Easter story with your children while you prepare meringue cookies together. Make this a family affair the Saturday night before Easter Sunday.

Ingredients:

1 cup pecan halves, to be broken

1 tsp. vinegar

3 egg whites

pinch of salt

1 cup of sugar

Gather the above ingredients, a Bible, and some adhesive tape. Preheat oven to 300 degrees and lightly grease a cookie sheet.

Place pecans in a plastic resealable bag. Give children wooden spoons and let them pound the pecans into small pieces. Set the bag aside. Explain that after Jesus was arrested, soldiers beat him. Read aloud John 19:1-3.

Let each helper smell the vinegar. Then measure 1 teaspoon into the mixing bowl. Explain that while dying on the cross, Jesus was thirsty and soldiers gave him vinegar to drink. Read John 19:29-30.

Separate the eggs. Add the whites to the vinegar. Eggs represent

I know that you are looking for Jesus, who was crucified. He is not here; he has risen, just as he said. *Come* and *see* the place where he lay. Then *go* quickly and *tell* his disciples: "He has risen from the dead."

Matthew 28:5-7 (NIV, emphasis added)

life. Explain that Jesus gave his life to give us life. Read aloud John 10:10-11,28.

Sprinkle a little salt into each person's palm and let each one brush it off into the mixture. Then they can taste their salty palms. This reminds us of salty tears shed by those saddened by Jesus' death. Read aloud Luke 23:27.

So far, the ingredients aren't very appetizing, but now sugar is added. Explain that the sweetest part of the story is that Jesus died because he loves us. He makes it possible to know him and to belong to him. Read aloud Psalm 34:8 and John 3:16.

Beat with electric mixer on high speed for 12 to 15 minutes until stiff peaks form. Point out the pearly white color, the color of purity, which is how God views those who have been cleansed from sin by Jesus' death. Read aloud Isaiah 1:18 and 1 John 3:1-3.

Fold in nuts. Drop teaspoons of the mixture on the cookie sheet. Explain that each mound resembles a rocky tomb like the one in which Jesus' body was placed. Read aloud Matthew 27:57-60.

Put the cookie sheet in the preheated oven, close the door, and turn the oven off completely. Hand each participant a piece of tape to secure the oven door. Explain that Jesus' tomb was sealed. Read aloud Matthew 27:65-66.

Explain that we may feel sad and disappointed to leave the cookies in the oven with the door closed. Likewise, Jesus' death seemed final to his followers, and they were in despair when the tomb was sealed. Read aloud John 16:20,22.

"One [Easter] I put a white ceramic angel that held a candle in each hand on the mantel over the fireplace. I will *never* forget coming upon our ten-year-old son, lying on the floor in the candle-lit darkness with his hands tucked under his head, meditating on the scene. When he became aware of my presence he said, '*Mom, look!!* It's just like the empty tomb and the angel is telling us, "He isn't here! The tomb is empty! He's risen from the dead!"'

"Well, sure enough! In the semidarkness the opening in the fireplace looked like an empty, dark hole. The radiant glow coming from the candles brought illumination of a special kind. One by one Rich called us all 'to come and see!'"[3]

—Martha Zimmerman, *Celebrating the Christian Year*

On Easter morning, open the oven door and give everyone a cookie. Point out the cracked surface of the cookies and then take a bite. The cookies are hollow! On the first Easter morning, Jesus' followers were amazed to find his tomb opened and empty. He had risen! Read aloud Matthew 28:1-9.[4]

RESURRECTION SUNDAY

When we have felt the weight of gloom on Thursday, Friday, and Saturday, we are more than ready on Sunday morning to celebrate the greatest news the world has ever heard: "Christ has indeed been raised from the dead"! (1 Corinthians 15:20, NIV).

- *A kite launch.* It's a custom in Bermuda to fly kites on Good Friday. This dates back to the nineteenth century when a teacher had trouble explaining Jesus' ascension into heaven. He brought his class to the highest hill on the island, where he launched a kite that had on it an image of Jesus. When the line ran out, he cut it, allowing it to float up to "heaven," and children have flown kites on Good Friday ever since.[6] So why not fly kites on Easter Sunday to celebrate the resurrection of Jesus or to talk about Jesus' final resurrection appearance, his ascension?

- *Balloon release.* On Saturday paint a large box with gray spray paint. Tell the children there will be a surprise on Sunday. After they have gone to bed, place a helium-filled balloon inside the gray box with a large rock on top. On Sunday take the family outside. Remove the rock and the box lid. Watch the balloon ascend and sing together the first verse of "Christ the Lord Is Risen Today."[7]

- *Butterfly release.* Purchase caterpillars from a science catalog or local natural science store about two weeks before Easter.

Easter is God's most astonishing miracle, the resurrection of Christ and the promise it holds for us—eternal life. A child who grasped this said, "Christmas is Jesus' birthday, but Easter is everybody's birthday."[5]

—Kathryn Slattery, *Guideposts*

Watch them spin cocoons, metamorphosing into butterflies. If the timing is right, release the butterflies on Resurrection Sunday. Explain that Jesus, lying in the grave, was like a caterpillar wrapped in a cocoon. After he died on the cross, men put his body in a cave and rolled a stone in front of it. But the cave could not hold him, just like the cocoon cannot hold the caterpillar. On that first Easter morning, Jesus came out of the cave alive, just as a butterfly emerges alive from the cocoon.

If you can't find caterpillars to purchase, make caterpillars by rolling pipe cleaners around pencils. Hang the caterpillars on an Easter tree. On Sunday morning, remove the caterpillars and replace them with butterflies made from wallpaper scraps or construction paper.

- *Sunrise service.* If your church doesn't have a sunrise service, have your own at home. Get up and dress before the sun is up. Then silently wait together in lawn chairs on the patio or on a blanket spread out on the living room floor. At the first hint of a sunbeam, sing "Christ Arose."

Our family likes to invite people to share our sunrise services with us. This occasion is too good to celebrate alone! We ask Christians to come because they understand the significance and share in our excitement, but we also invite non-Christians—"Come see how crazy we are!"

Our patio faces the morning sun, and we gather there to watch the sun come up behind three crosses built by our son Ben. We sing songs, share our experiences of God's goodness, and sing joyfully as the morning opens before us. What a wonderful experience!

From the joy of Palm Sunday, to the mystery of the Last Supper, to the darkness of the Crucifixion, and finally to the joy of Easter morning—the opportunities to worship and celebrate are many and wonderful! Enjoy—and grow in your knowledge of the Lord as you do!

THE LEGEND OF THE RED EGGS

"Dye some eggs red to recall the legend of the first Easter eggs. The legend tells us that Mary Magdalene went to Pontius Pilate on Easter morning to tell him of the Resurrection. She brought him a gift of eggs. Pilate refused the gift and said he would not believe Jesus had risen unless the eggs turned red. In an instant the eggs turned red and Pilate believed!"[8]

—Jeanne Hunt, *Holy Bells and Wonderful Smells*

CHAPTER 5

OH SAY, CAN YOU SEE WAYS TO CELEBRATE LIBERTY?

The Fourth of July

On the anniversary of the day in 1776 when the American colonies declared their independence from England, we can celebrate our nation's freedom, reaffirm patriotism and other democratic values, encourage loyalty to our country, and express our faith. Day by day we're apt to focus more often on what is wrong with our country than on what is right. We complain about spiritual apathy, immorality, drugs, crime, healthcare, and homelessness—real problems that need effective solutions. But if we pause to consider and celebrate what is right with the United States, perhaps we will be inspired to combat some of its ills. The July Fourth holiday gives us the perfect opportunity to do just that.

OUR DECLARATION OF INDEPENDENCE

In the early days of our country, England ruled the colonies from across the sea, disgruntling many colonists. They were particularly upset by taxation without representation: Their taxes kept increasing, and they had no representatives in England's Parliament to express their point of view. Their unrest and discontent growing, the colonists formed a committee to compose a formal declaration of independence. On July 2, 1776, the delegates of the colonies voted for independence. On July 4, 1776, they signed the Declaration of Independence and a new nation, the United States of America, was born.

What better way to remember this important historical moment than by highlighting the Declaration of Independence sometime during the Fourth of July holiday? Here are some ideas for how you can do this. (Although children who can't yet read will not be able to actively participate in some of these activities, they will catch the flavor of the moment as the whole group makes the Declaration of Independence its own.)

- Have someone give a dramatic reading of the Declaration of Independence or portions of it.

- Provide copies of the Declaration of Independence for everyone. Take turns reading it aloud, paragraph by paragraph or sentence by sentence.

- Print on place cards the most famous sentence from the Declaration of Independence: "We hold these Truths to be self-evident, that all Men are created equal, that they are endowed by their Creator with certain unalienable Rights, that among these are Life, Liberty, and the Pursuit of Happiness." Before the blessing, ask family members and/or guests to read this line together. Afterward you might say something like this: "When they were written, these words expressed a bold idea. Before then, most people believed that the government granted them whatever rights they had. It is important that, like the forefathers of our country, we acknowledge where our

The central role of Christianity in the birth and development of America is documented by substantial historical evidence. In 1994, U. S. Supreme Court Justice Earl Warren said, "I believe no one can read the history of our country...without realizing that the Good Book and the spirit of the Savior have from the beginning been our guiding geniuses."[1]
—James Muffett, *Light and Life*

rights come from and that we do all we can to preserve them. As we thank God for our meal, let's also thank him for the rights he grants us."

• Excerpt lines from the Declaration of Independence and read them as a group. When I did this, I printed the following lines on pieces of stiff white paper, rolled the paper, tied each with a red ribbon, and placed one at each plate at a Fourth of July barbecue. Before my husband asked the blessing on our barbecue, our family and guests read the following:

Bob: When in the Course of human Events,

Susan: it becomes necessary for one People to dissolve the Political Bands that have connected them with another,

Dave: and to assume among the Powers of the Earth,

Ray: the separate and equal Station to which the Laws of Nature and of Nature's God entitle them,

Gerry: a decent Respect to the Opinions of Mankind requires that they should declare the causes that impel them to the Separation.

THE DECLARATION OF INDEPENDENCE CONTAINS FOUR REFERENCES TO GOD:

1. "and to assume among the Powers of the Earth, the separate and equal Station to which the Laws of Nature and of Nature's God entitle them"

2. "We hold these Truths to be self-evident, that all Men are created equal, that they are endowed by their Creator with certain unalienable Rights."

3. "appealing to the Supreme Judge of the World, for the Rectitude of our Intentions"

4. "with a firm Reliance on the Protection of divine Providence"

All: We hold these Truths to be self-evident, that all Men are created equal, that they are endowed by their Creator with certain unalienable Rights, that among these are Life, Liberty, and the Pursuit of Happiness.

- Give each person a copy of the Declaration of Independence. Ask them to look for references to God while they are waiting for the hamburgers to grill. Before the blessing or between the main course and dessert, ask them to share their discoveries.

RING THE LIBERTY BELL

Americans treasure the Liberty Bell, which hangs in Independence Hall in Philadelphia and symbolizes our freedom. Colonists rang this bell in 1776 to announce the signing of the Declaration of Independence. The inscription on the Liberty Bell says, in part, "Proclaim liberty throughout the land."

- Ring a bell when calling your guests to eat their grilled hamburgers and potato salad. Say, "Let's proclaim our liberty! Praise God we are free!"

- Hang your own "Liberty Bell" from a ceiling. If you have small children, have them take turns ringing the bell. If they are too short to reach the cord, have them throw beans bags or rolled socks to make the bell ring.

PRAISE OUR NATION'S LEADERS

We Americans would not have the freedom and quality of life we enjoy if it were not for courageous men and women who were influential at pivotal points in our history. Celebrate the Fourth by

SCRIPTURES ABOUT LIBERTY

Read Bible verses about liberty at breakfast on the Fourth of July or when your family and friends gather for a picnic.

Leviticus 25:10

Psalm 119:45

John 8:32

1 Corinthians 7:22

Galatians 5:1

1 Peter 2:15-16

remembering some of these important people—and add your own heroes to the list.

- Find an adult who will happily impersonate Paul Revere, George Washington, Thomas Jefferson, Abraham Lincoln, Uncle Sam, Betsy Ross, or Martin Luther King Jr. Invite him or her to join your July Fourth picnic and deliver a short patriotic address or a monologue about his or her character.

- Place some coins on the table around your Fourth of July centerpiece. Note the coins before you say grace. Say something like this: "Every coin minted in the United States has these words: 'Liberty' and 'In God We Trust.' Our forefathers knew the great sacrifices and tremendous cost paid to secure our freedom. In gratitude they continually acknowledged that God had made and preserved our nation. They sought his help in all that they did.[2] Let's thank God today for our forefathers and ask him to help us continue to be a nation that trusts in him."

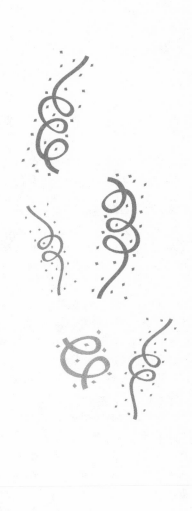

- Ask each person to write on a Post-it note the name of a famous person involved in shaping and building our nation. Collect the Post-it notes in a basket. Pass the basket around and have all participants take out a Post-it note and put it on another person's forehead for everyone to see. Have participants try to guess the name they have on their forehead by asking yes-or-no questions such as "Was this person a military hero?" or "Is this person remembered for her words?" or "Is this person remembered for____?" The first person to guess correctly should get some prize like getting served dessert first or not having to help clean up the dishes.

WHERE DID UNCLE SAM COME FROM?

Did you ever wonder where Uncle Sam came from? A man named Sam Wilson, who lived in Troy, New York, dealt with army supplies during the War of 1812. He was called Uncle Sam by many people in his community, and one of his workers said jokingly that the initials U. S. (for United States) that were stamped on each barrel of army supplies really stood for "Uncle Sam." Soon the expression became popular, as soldiers talked about fighting Uncle Sam's war and eating Uncle Sam's meat in the army. Sam Wilson probably didn't look anything like the tall, thin, bearded figure in striped clothes that was drawn later in the nineteenth century by the cartoonist Thomas Nast. But his name is still famous today.[3]

—Carol Barkin and Elizabeth James,
The Holiday Handbook

- People of all ages who are unfamiliar with American history can play a game similar to "Twenty Questions." Assign participants (including children) the name of a famous patriotic person a few days before your gathering. This will give them some time to learn about the historical figure. Then, at your July Fourth celebration, guests can take turns asking the other participants yes-or-no questions to figure out who they are. Questions might include, "Did this person live before 1776?" "Was this person a man?" "Was this person associated with writing the Declaration of Independence?" The group can ask each person who has a mystery name up to twenty questions.

HAVE YOUR OWN PARADE

Everyone loves a parade, especially children. So invite the children in your neighborhood or church to have a parade with their bikes, wagons, skates, and strollers. You can make this a spur-of-the-moment affair or let people know a week or so in advance. Either way, kids (and adults!) enjoy expressing their patriotism in a parade.

Make a parade banner on a large sheet of butcher paper. With red and blue markers, write "Thank God for Freedom" or "God Bless America." Choose two people to hold the banner and lead the parade.

Have the kids decorate their bicycles, tricycles, riding toys, and wagons with red, white, and blue streamers, balloons, and ribbons. They could even make some star-spangled cardboard license plates for their "vehicles."

Some children may want to dress in red, white, and blue or wear a costume in the parade. The Fourth of July inspires lots of possibilities for costumes with patriotic themes. With striped pants, a tailcoat, and a cardboard top hat, anyone can march as Uncle Sam. For simpler fun, just dab on red, white, and blue face paint. Use water-based face paint to draw stars, eagles, and flags on cheeks, noses, and foreheads.

Of course, no parade would be complete without music. Put a portable CD/cassette player in a wagon and play band music and lots of John Philip Sousa marches. Let younger children beat an old pan with a spoon or shake a bunch of metal measuring spoons for a tinkling sound. Make drums out of empty oatmeal boxes or coffee cans. Put some uncooked macaroni or dry beans between two paper plates, staple the plates together, and you'll have tambourines. Decorate them with streaming ribbons or crayon drawings.[4] Give small American flags to those children who don't have an instrument to play or a vehicle to ride.

Hold your parade where other people can watch. March around the backyard while Dad finishes barbecuing. If you're more ambitious, march around the block or up and down the street. If several families are picnicking in the park, take your parade there.

End the parade with everyone singing "God Bless America."

KEEP AMERICA SINGING

In the shower or car, in a chorus, at a birthday party, at church, or most anyplace, singing is often an act of celebration. And singing

A SIMPLE CRAFT

No Fourth of July parade would be complete without a drum! Add to the fun by making your own. Let children decide how to decorate their drums to reflect their impressions of the holiday.

Start with empty cylinder-shaped containers (salt or oatmeal boxes work well, as do coffee or shortening cans). Provide an assortment of decorating supplies, including red, white, and blue construction paper; red, white, or blue paint with brushes; star shapes; patriotic stickers; pieces of fabric; glitter; heavy string or yarn; scissors; and glue.

Paint the container or cover it with fabric or construction paper. Poke a hole on opposite sides of the cylinder and run a long piece of heavy string or yarn through the can, tying the ends of the string together so the child can hang the drum around his or her neck. (If you're using a coffee can, you will need to use a hammer and a large nail to make the holes.)

Decorate the sides of the drum with stars, glitter, colored stripes of material or construction paper, or stickers—whatever the child's imagination calls for! There's no limit to the creative possibilities.

For the drumsticks you could

- use long metal or wooden spoons,
- make a slight slit in a small rubber ball and push a pencil or 1/4-inch dowel inside, or
- cover the ends of pencils or sticks with white cloth padded with tissue.

Now you're ready to drum away!

JUST A PIECE OF CLOTH

That's all it is...just a piece of cloth.

You can count the threads in it, and it's no different from any other piece of cloth.

But then a little breeze comes along, and it stirs and comes to life and flutters and snaps in the wind, all red, white and blue.

It has your whole life wrapped up in it... the meals you're going to eat...the time you're going to spend with your spouse...the kind of things your child will learn at school...those strange and wonderful thoughts you get inside a church on Sunday.

Those stars in it...they make you feel just as free as the stars in the wide, deep night. And those stripes...they're bars of blood to any dictator who'd try to change it.

Just a piece of cloth, that's all it is...until you put your soul in it and give it meaning.

What do you want to make it mean? A symbol of liberty and decency and fair-dealing for everyone?

Then, let's do something about it. Let's do *plenty* and do it *soon enough.*

Yes, that flag is just a piece of cloth until we breathe life into it. Until we make it stand for everything we believe in and refuse to live without.[5]

—Anonymous

songs that exalt God and country may be just the patriotic touch your Fourth of July gathering needs. Here are some suggestions:

"America the Beautiful"

"Mine Eyes Have Seen the Glory"

"The Star-Spangled Banner"

"America" ("My Country 'Tis of Thee")

"God Bless America"

"God Bless the USA"

"This Land Is Your Land"

"Lift Every Voice and Sing"

"God of Our Fathers"

In order to sing these songs with the gusto they deserve, provide copies of the words for your guests. After all, how many times have you started to sing "The Star-Spangled Banner" and found you could only remember a few lines?

RALLY 'ROUND THE FLAG

On the Fourth of July, America's Stars and Stripes are proudly displayed across the nation, from all public buildings and from many homes and businesses. So, if you have a big flag, display it. If you don't, get some small flags and tie a bunch to your mailbox or put some in an outdoor flowerpot.

- Make a ceremony out of displaying the flag. Ask those in your celebration circle to say the Pledge of Allegiance. Follow that with a brief prayer of gratitude for the freedom you enjoy as an American.

- If you have small children, talk with them about why we fly the flag on our country's birthday. Encourage them to tell about where they have seen the American flag displayed. Ask them to name the colors of the flag. Talk about the significance of the flag's colors: Red symbolizes hardiness, courage, and shed blood; white stands for purity and innocence; and blue means vigilance, perseverance, and justice.

- Have someone give a dramatic reading of the essay "Just a Piece of Cloth," or provide copies for everyone to read aloud together.

Blest with vict'ry and peace,
  may the heav'n-rescued land
Praise the Pow'r that hath made
  and preserved us a nation!
Then conquer we must,
  when our cause it is just,
And this be our motto:
  "In God is our trust!"
          —from the third stanza
    of "The Star-Spangled Banner,"
          by Francis Scott Key

Don't let the Fourth of July be just a national holiday! Use the opportunity to thank God, the giver of all good gifts, for the gift of this country and the freedoms you enjoy as a citizen.

CHAPTER 6

SHINING LIGHT INTO HALLOWEEN'S DARKNESS

Halloween

Have you noticed how extreme reactions to Halloween can be? Some people plunge in and embrace all of the pagan symbolism of the holiday: ghouls and ghosts, witches, black cats, and evil spirits. Others, however, regard the day as totally evil and want nothing to do with it. Yet there is much about Halloween that children and adults enjoy, such as partying and wearing costumes. Why not capitalize on this enjoyment by looking for the good and inserting *meaning* into the celebration?

WHERE'S THE GOOD?

What Christian values and beliefs can we connect with Halloween?

The goodness of God. During Halloween we can celebrate God's goodness. When supermarkets, roadside stands, and garden centers put out colorful pumpkins and gourds, we can rejoice over God's creative work. Leaves of crimson, amber, and yellow add their touch of fall beauty to his creation. Orange pumpkins, red apples, multicolored squash, and dried cornstalks remind us of bountiful harvests and God's generous providence.

Our Christian history. Halloween blends pagan customs and religious practices. The pagan came first. Festivals involving evil spirits and malicious tricks were held on the last day of October in honor of the sun god and to mark the beginning of a new year.

In the fourth century, Christians

Why allow Halloween to be a pagan holiday in commemoration of the powers of darkness? Fill the house or church with light: sing and celebrate the victory of Christ over darkness.[1]
—Richard Foster, *Celebration of Discipline*

began honoring all the saints with festivals. Eventually this annual May celebration was called All Hallows Day (*hallow* comes from the word *holy*). As the celebration grew in popularity, having enough food became a problem, so the feast was moved to November 1, when the fall harvest would provide an abundant supply of food. The evening before, October 31, became known as All Hallows Eve or Halloween.[2] So, at Halloween, we can focus on All Hallows Day or All Saints Day and celebrate our rich heritage of faith by remembering believers who have gone before us and thanking God for their example.

People of authenticity. At Halloween, when children and adults playfully masquerade as someone or something else, we can talk about how Christianity encourages authenticity. People look on the outward appearance—the face being shown to the world—but God looks on the heart (1 Samuel 16:7). Jesus died for us just as we are; we didn't have to dress ourselves up first (Romans 5:6,8). Then, forgiven and filled with the Holy Spirit, we are to make sure our actions reflect the nature of our heavenly Father (1 John 3:18, Matthew 5:21–6:18, Galatians 5:16,22-23 and Ephesians 4:17–5:21).

People of light. Many of Halloween's pagan customs point to darkness, death, and evil. As people of light and life, Christians have power over evil. We believe in Jesus, who described himself as the Light of the World (John 8:12 and 9:5) and the Resurrection and the Life (John 11:25). Jesus taught us that light can penetrate the darkness, and he said to his followers, "You are the light of the world" (Matthew 5:14-16, NIV). Halloween is a perfect time to recognize that we are people of light, called to walk in the Light.

So the question is, how can we celebrate these good things at Halloween?

INSTEAD OF "TRICK OR TREAT," "GIVE AND GREET"

Masquerading gives us a chance to be creative, and it gives other people the fun of guessing who we are. But "trick or treating" can all too easily become an exercise in greed. Why not encourage your family to "give and greet" instead of "trick or treat"? Parents and kids alike can dress up in costumes and visit older adults who are homebound or living in retirement centers and nursing homes. If they know you, let them guess who you are. If you visit people who don't know you, have a parade for them. You might ask them to guess what character you are representing. Give those you visit a cookie or an apple with an encouraging Bible verse attached. Brightening the lives of others like this is one way we can be the people of light we are called to be.

TAKE A TRIP TO A PUMPKIN FARM OR A COUNTRY MARKET

Pumpkins can be grown in most soil conditions and in regions with shorter growing seasons. Every pioneer farmer planted this reliable crop. Ripening throughout the fall, pumpkins kept for a long time in a cool cellar. When other crops failed to produce enough to help them survive the winter, families could count on pumpkins to get them through.

In the midst of a field of pumpkins we can bask in fall's bounty and acknowledge God's goodness.

GOOD BOOKS FOR KIDS (AGES 4-8)

- *The Pumpkin Patch Parable* by Liz Curtis Higgs: A farmer (God) reaches down, picks out a special pumpkin from his garden, and scoops out all the messy goo to make room for his light to shine through.

- *Halloween, Is It for Real?* by Harold Lawrence Myra: Children make plans for a fun-filled Halloween harvest festival—complete with costumes, games, pumpkins, and popcorn—as they discover how early Christians celebrated All Hallows Day as an affirmation of God's victory over evil and death.

- Find a pumpkin for each member of the family—a tiny one for the baby, a tall oval one for Dad, etc. Work together to carve a face on each one. When you finish, place candles in the pumpkins and talk about how each of us can let our light shine for Jesus. Stand back, admire your work, and sing together "This Little Light of Mine."

- Buy two pumpkins. Work together to carve a happy face in one and a sad or angry face in the other. Light a candle in each and turn out the lights. Look at the differences between the happy pumpkin face and the sad one. Decide together which is the best face and why. You might talk about how faces reveal inner feelings. Also mention how our smiles and laughter can make the people around us less sad.

- Put a large candle in a carved or, if you prefer, ceramic jack-o-lantern. Darken the room and light the candle. Watch the flame as it fills the pumpkin and lights the room. As the light of the pumpkin illuminates the room, talk about how the light of Jesus penetrates the darkness. Sing together "Shine, Jesus, Shine."

HAVE A PUMPKIN-DECORATING PARTY

Invite people to your home for a Halloween party. In the invitation, tell your guests that each household will be decorating (as opposed to carving) a pumpkin. Explain that you will furnish the pumpkins, but

TRICK-OR-TREAT FOR UNICEF

In 1950, a new Halloween custom began. Members of a youth group in Philadelphia collected money for poor children all around the world. When they went trick-or-treating, they carried empty milk cartons and asked for money. They collected $17.

The money was given to UNICEF, the United Nations International Children's Emergency Fund. UNICEF helps children all over the world who are hungry, poor, or sick. Soon, many children were trick-or-treating for UNICEF.

U.S. President Lyndon Johnson officially recognized the trick-or-treat for UNICEF program in 1967. Today, children trick-or-treating for UNICEF carry special cartons.[3]

—Martin Hintz and Kate Hintz, *Halloween: Why We Celebrate It the Way We Do*

they are to bring their own ideas and supplies. Ask them not to buy decorative items, but instead to look around their house—from the refrigerator to the sewing basket—for things they can use that they already have.

As an alternative approach, keep the pumpkin-decorating a surprise. Have trays of items that can be used for decorating: mop heads, vegetables, hats, candy (licorice ropes for hair, gumdrops for eyes, marshmallows for noses), eye glasses—anything that can be pinned or glued to the pumpkin.

At the party give each household a pumpkin to decorate with the items they brought or you provided. When the decorating is complete, have everyone vote by secret ballot for the best one, and give a prize to the winning group. Serve refreshments and then end the party with some devotional thoughts (see ideas suggested previously in this chapter in "Where's the Good?").

Decorating pumpkins rather than carving them has its bonuses. Gone is the danger and mess of carving and scooping. With the knife out of the way, children of almost any age can participate in a pumpkin project. And when the party is over, the uncarved pumpkin can be cooked and used for pie or bread!

HOST A COSTUME PARTY

Ask guests to come dressed as men and women from the Bible or Christian history for a "When the Saints Come Marching In" Party. Some churches will actually have a list of saints, people who are officially recognized for unusual holiness. If yours does not, look back at

The custom of making jack-o-lanterns began in the Old World. Children carved their jack-o-lanterns out of large turnips and put candles inside them. When families moved to America, they found pumpkins readily available and substituted them for turnips. It's not hard to see why. Have you ever tried to hollow out a turnip?

To cook pumpkin, wash it and cut it in half, crosswise. Remove the seeds and strings. Place the pieces of pumpkin in a pan, shell side up, and bake in a 325-degree oven for one hour or more, depending on size, until the pumpkin is tender and begins to fall apart. Scrape the pulp from the shell and put it through a ricer or strainer.[4] Now you have pulp for making your favorite pie or bread.

—*The Joy of Cooking*

church history and identify those people who courageously lived out their faith or were extraordinarily righteous.

If you have invited young children or guests with a limited knowledge of Christian history, either keep the costumes limited to Bible characters or send a brief description of a Christian saint and ask the person to come dressed in character. Joan of Arc, Charles Wesley, John Wesley, Lottie Moon, Corrie ten Boom, Martin Luther, Francis of Assisi, William Carey, Adoniram Judson, and John the Baptist are some saints to choose from.

If you have a lot of kids at your party, announce each character when he or she arrives and then have that character march around the room with "When the Saints Go Marching In" playing in the background. After everyone arrives, ask guests to guess who is behind the costume.

If you want your costumed guests to mingle as they arrive, pin a large number on each one. Have all the guests register by writing down the name of their character and their own name next to the number they were assigned. Provide each guest with a piece of paper and a pencil so they can record their guesses about who their fellow saints are as they ask yes-or-no questions. Give prizes for the best costumes, to the one who identifies the most saints, and to the person who identifies the most impersonators.

Another approach to a masquerade party is to have your guests make costumes after they arrive. Have plenty of old clothes, sheets, wigs, glasses, and make-up on hand and see how creative your guests can be. You could divide guests into groups and have them design a costume and dress up one person in the group. Have a parade where the "dressed" person walks around the room, displaying his or her costume. Give prizes and applause to the group who does the best.

Masquerade parties like these offer a great opportunity for emphasizing the importance of authenticity. So close with devotional thoughts about the masks we are tempted to wear and reminders that Jesus often denounced hypocrisy. (The word *hypocrite* means a pretender, one who acts a part, one who wears a mask to cover his true feelings, one who puts on an external show while inwardly his thoughts and feelings are very different.) Close with a prayer, thanking God that he loves us just as we are.

THROW A HARVEST PARTY

Plan an outdoor party and schedule it in the late afternoon so there will be enough daylight for two harvest hunts.

- Ask guests to come dressed as their favorite season of the year. They can use cotton balls, construction paper, dyed sheets, tree branches, and tinsel to make their costumes. My friend Judy asked her guests to do this, and she said, "Several came with leaves all over them. Others chose to dress up as rain, snow, and a cold winter's night. They were so creative!"

- Have a treasure hunt, forming teams and assigning each one a specific color. Give team members one clue. The first clue will guide them to the second one, the second clue to the third one, and so on. If a team stumbles upon a clue of a different color, they should leave it alone; they can neither take it nor tell others where it was hidden.

  Sample clues include:

  "This clue is caged"—a birdcage on the patio
  "The flag's up on this one"—a clue in the mailbox
  "You're hot when you find this pot"—a clue in flowerpot

  Give the same tenth clue to everyone, guiding the hunters to buried treasure hidden under a pile of leaves. Use a small box designed to look like a pirate's chest to hold the treasure (prizes and candy for the team members to share).

- Have a scavenger hunt. Give each team a grocery sack and tell them to go from house to house collecting items associated with fall. Set a thirty-minute time limit and a neighborhood boundary line. You might assign certain areas for each team so that neighbors won't get bombarded with requests. Hunters should return with all sorts of things: autumn flowers, pine cones, corn stalks, assorted leaves, and nuts.

- As darkness begins to fall, gather guests around a fire and roast hot dogs and marshmallows. After dinner, sit around the fire. Sing songs and end with comments about the beauty of God's creation and a prayer of thanks for God's goodness.

Be light in the darkness! Redeem the pagan aspects of Halloween by focusing on the God-given bounty of fall and the rich heritage of the saints who have gone before you.

A GREAT PUMPKIN HUNT

Build a giant pumpkin out of papier-mâché or purchase a large pumpkin that can be hidden in the yard. Guests can follow clues in the same manner as the treasure hunt. The team that gets to the Great Pumpkin first and brings it back will be the winner.

CHAPTER 7

LET EVERYONE GIVE THANKS

Thanksgiving

In the United States we celebrate Thanksgiving on the fourth Thursday of November. Even though we trace Thanksgiving back to the Pilgrims of the early 1600s, this celebration didn't become a national holiday until 1863, thanks in great part to Sara Josepha Hale. One of the country's first female editors, beginning with *Ladies Magazine* in Boston and then *Godey's Lady's Book* in Philadelphia, she wrote editorials for forty years, urging that we, as a nation, set aside a specific day to give thanks.

Finally, President Abraham Lincoln issued a Thanksgiving proclamation, and we've been giving thanks together in November ever since.[1]

LET EVERYONE SAY THANKS

With Thanksgiving weekend including school breaks, travel, eating turkey, hunting deer, and watching football, it's easy to forget to be thankful. To encourage grateful hearts all around the Thanksgiving dinner table, choose one of the following activities instead of having one person say a general prayer of thanks.

- *Symbolic kernels.* Put a leaf (a real one you have pressed ahead of time, an artificial one bought at a craft store, or one cut from construction paper) beside each person's plate. On each, place five kernels of corn. When everyone is

The Puritans refused to celebrate Christmas. They would not allow so much as a mincemeat pie on Christmas Day, but even they felt the need to offer thanksgiving. Community and congregational thanksgiving days were declared for special causes: the end of an epidemic, rainfall after a drought, and victory in war. These thanksgiving days were days of prayer followed by "making merry" at family dinners where mincemeat pie became a part of the menu![2]

—Diana Karter Appelbaum,
adapted from *Thanksgiving:
An American Holiday, An American History*

What do "Mary Had a Little Lamb" and Thanksgiving have in common? The woman we have to thank for our Thanksgiving holiday, Sara Josepha Hale, also wrote "Mary Had a Little Lamb."

seated, say something like this, "After finally arriving in a land where they had religious freedom, the Pilgrims faced the challenge of surviving their first winter here. Sickness struck hard, and starvation was a very real possibility. Some historians say that they were rationed just five kernels of corn per meal. Half of the community died. Fortunately spring came early, but it was followed by a long summer of hard work. In the fall the Pilgrims were blessed with a bountiful harvest. The colony would survive! In celebration of that harvest, they held a great feast in October 1621 and gave thanks to God. Let the five kernels of corn by your plate remind you of our past and present. Let's express our thanks today by naming five things for which we are thankful." Pass a basket around and ask each person to drop the five kernels of corn in the basket one at a time, naming five things he or she is thankful for.[3]

• *Colorful leaves.* On a table place large leaves made out of yellow, brown, and orange construction paper. Set markers and a basket nearby. As guests arrive, ask them to write some things they are thankful for on the leaves and drop them in the basket. As you serve dessert, bring the basket to the table with you. One by one, take the leaves out of the basket and read aloud the words of thanksgiving.

Or, after the main course give each guest some markers and brightly colored paper leaves with strings attached. While family members clear the table and prepare dessert, ask guests to write what they are thankful for on the leaves. Then have the children decorate your Thanksgiving Tree (a leafless branch anchored in plaster of Paris) by hanging the leaves on it. As you serve dessert say, "See how thankful we are!" Ask the older children to read what is written on some of the leaves.

- *Harmonizing prayer.* You may want to opt for a short prayer. Put a printed, easy-to-say prayer by each place setting. Ask everyone to repeat the prayer together as an expression of gratitude. Here are two short prayers:

> "Blessed art Thou, O Lord, our God,
> King of the World,
> who brings forth bread from the earth
> and who blesses us abundantly."

> "In these moments before we eat,
> we are mindful of all we have
>   for which we give you thanks:
> friends, food, hopes, health and happy memories.
> In giving thanks, we are blessed,
> and we pray you are blessed, too."

And to follow is one more prayer. It's by Dag Hammarskjold, a former United Nations secretary-general. These two short

You can make your Thanksgiving experience even richer by beginning your "thanks collection" weeks ahead. Karen O'Connor and her husband began in January. Using a silver foil gift bag, they labeled it "Our Blessing Bag" and set it on a table in their bedroom. They placed a pad of paper and pen beside it for writing down their blessings to deposit in the bag.

As the new year began, they started recording their blessings. By November, their container was "full to overflowing"—and so were their hearts after they read all that they had written. On Thanksgiving morning they propped themselves up in bed and dumped out the slips of paper. They read aloud the blessings they had described. Karen said that it was a joy to read what they were thankful for and to take notice of how God had blessed them in the previous months. She said, "By the time we got to the last scrap of paper we were in tears. How could we ever again doubt that God provides for our every need and protects our going out and coming in!"[4]

lines say so much. His prayer would be good at the beginning or end of a traditional Thanksgiving meal:

"For all that has been—Thanks!
To all that shall be—Yes!"[5]

- *Prayerful walk.* When the kitchen gets all steamy from the turkey baking in the oven, our family likes to get outdoors, take a walk, and pray. We walk beside each other, shoulder to shoulder. We designate a place to begin praying and a place where we will stop. (Having a designated beginning and end makes everyone more comfortable.) My husband opens the prayer time and thanks God for one specific item, and then I pray, followed by our eldest son, Jim, then our middle son, Joel, and ending with our youngest son, Ben. After Ben prays, Bob prays again, thanking God for another specific item, and we all take turns again. We continue this as we walk. If a person is finished, he says, "I pass" when his turn comes, and the rest of us continue to take turns praying. When we get to our designated ending spot, I close the prayer of thanks.

- *Group praise.* Read responsively a thanks-and-praise liturgy right before the Thanksgiving meal. We have often used Psalms 100 and 145 at our home. These two psalms, along with Psalm 103, offer lots of ideas. And you can expand any of them. Here's one based on Psalm 100 (NIV):

  Husband: *Family and friends,*
  Make a joyful noise to the Lord!

  Wife: *Serve the Lord with gladness!*
  Come into his presence with enthusiasm!

A NOVEL THANKSGIVING EXERCISE

Instead of giving a round of thanks for what you have, thank God for what you don't have or for what didn't happen. This exercise will definitely raise your Gratitude Quotient.

"I am thankful that when I forgot and left the candle burning in the bathroom, my house did not burn down."

"I am thankful that when the brakes failed on my car, I was at a place where I could pull over and not be hit by oncoming traffic."

"Although I live in tornado alley, I thank God I don't have to worry about earthquakes or mudslides."

"I thank God for every time I have tripped over my son's ball glove and my daughter's skates because I'm reminded I have a family, and that makes me happy."

It is a good thing to give thanks unto the LORD.

Psalm 92:1

A SIMPLE DRAMA

Read the story of the ten lepers (Luke 17:11-19). Remind your children that Jesus was pleased with the one man who returned to give thanks for being healed. Provide rags for bandages and let your children play the roles of the lepers and Jesus.[6]

Lettie Kirkpatrick, *Christian Parenting Today*

All: *Know that the Lord is God!*
              It is he who made us, and we are his;
              we are his people,
              and the sheep of his pasture.

Husband: *Partake of this meal with thanksgiving,*
              and offer God your praise!

Wife: *Give thanks to him,*
              bless his name!

All: *For the Lord is good;*
              his steadfast love endures forever,
              and his faithfulness to all generations.

LET THE CHILDREN SAY THANKS

Children can get rambunctious and restless as they wait for the big meal. Channel that energy by creatively guiding their thoughts toward being thankful. The results can help the whole group find Thanksgiving more meaningful.

- Tape record the thanksgiving of small children. Ask someone to take them to another room and ask them, one by one, what they are thankful for. Away from the adults, their thanks will be more heartfelt and honest. Play the tape between the main course and the dessert.

- Have children practice saying or singing the poem "Mary Had a Little Lamb" together. Ask them to recite it right before the meal or between the meal and dessert. Follow their rendition by telling about Sara Josepha Hale, the woman who campaigned for our Thanksgiving holiday.

- Have a long piece of newsprint and many different colored washable markers available. Assign each child a section of the newsprint. Let them draw or write on the mural what they are thankful for. Tape the mural to the wall before dinner. At dinner have the children explain what they drew ("Tell us what you're thankful for").

Ways to Encourage Gratitude

Just because a holiday arrives right on schedule doesn't mean that we will be in the mood to celebrate. Our moods don't always correspond to the holiday! I learned that truth the year my husband invited the women and children from a shelter for abused women to be our guests for Thanksgiving dinner. Bob was their Bible study teacher, and he didn't want them to spend Thanksgiving at the shelter. I wholeheartedly agreed.

On the Wednesday night before Thanksgiving, our family attended a worship service at our church. The pastor asked us to say what we were thankful for. I didn't volunteer. If he had asked me specifically to respond, I would have obliged, giving the standard reply: "I'm thankful for my family, my friends, food, health, and shelter." But somehow I didn't really feel thankful so I said nothing.

The next day our guests came. Bob knew them from his weekly class, but I didn't. As I met them, I couldn't help but be struck by the evident hurt and abuse in their faces. I hadn't realized how visible their pain would be. I was struck, too, by the listlessness of their conversation. We ate dinner together and played outside games. To anyone passing by, we looked like a large family gathering. But the women were painfully aware of what was missing from their lives.

After the games, Bob gathered everyone in our family room. I'm sure they expected a lesson on Thanksgiving, but Bob surprised them. He said, "Today is a day to give thanks. I want to go around the room and have everyone say something they are thankful for."

When Bob said this, the group fell apart. Suddenly everyone had to check on a child, go to the bathroom, or have a cigarette. But no one said, "Excuse me" or "I'm sorry I have to go." They simply left the room.

Later, after our guests had returned to the shelter, Bob and I cleaned the kitchen. Bob said, "As soon as I voiced the request, I knew I had said the wrong thing. I never thought anything about it. Everyone has something to be thankful for. They can be thankful they're an American."

But the pain these women knew was so great that they simply could not voice any thanks. Suddenly I realized that I could. My emotions caught up with the calendar, and I took a long prayerful walk. Floods of gratitude poured over me: "Thank you, God, for the shelter of a home. Thank you, God, for a wonderful husband and a secure marriage. Thank you for children who have never known abuse…" The list went on and on. Through that experience of contrasting my life with someone else's, my emotions were moved so that I could celebrate Thanksgiving in the true sense of the word.

Here are some ways all of us can encourage gratitude in others and foster it in ourselves, so that we give thanks from our hearts, not just with our words.

- Invite guests whose lives (like those women from the shelter) may contrast sharply with yours: lonely people, international students, unemployed folks, those with recent loss, people of a different economic level, or newcomers to your community.

- Serve rice and water for the evening meal the night before Thanksgiving Day. Eat it by candlelight. This sparse meal will remind family members of those people around the world who are hungry and who live without electricity.

- Volunteer as a family to help prepare and/or serve Thanksgiving dinner at a local homeless shelter or the Salvation Army.

- Share the story of the Pilgrims' first Thanksgiving celebration. In a variation of the five kernels activity mentioned earlier, give each hungry diner five kernels of cooked corn before you bring the food to your decorated table. Encourage everyone to eat the corn. Then ask, "Do you feel satisfied? Are you ready to leave the table?" As you discuss their empty feelings after such a small meal, talk about these questions: "What would we do if there was no more food?" "What might real hunger feel like?" "Where in our world, our country, our city do families leave their table hungry?"[7]

- Cook a complete Thanksgiving meal for a needy family and deliver it on Thanksgiving Day.

- Even something as simple as a short walk on a cold day or night can remind us that we have many reasons to be thankful. A little discomfort helps us realize how comfortable we are and how important those comforts are to us. With a little discomfort or a little contrast, we can *feel* grateful as well as *say* we are grateful.

Giving thanks is always in season, but it's especially appropriate in the harvest month of November. Let's have fun with thanks, fresh and leftover, traditional and innovative. After all, we know from whom all blessings flow, so as the psalmist said, "Give thanks to the LORD, for he is good" (Psalm 107:1, NIV).

WHAT TO DO WITH THE LEFTOVERS?

Invite college students home for the Thanksgiving weekend or ask friends whom you haven't seen for a while to visit for a Leftover Party on the Friday after Thanksgiving. Ask guests to:

- bring leftover food from their Thursday Thanksgiving feast

- wear leftover clothes: something old and comfortable like jeans or sweats instead of anything new

- bring a leftover game (one from your childhood) to share with the group

- bring a leftover thanks, one you didn't share on Thanksgiving Day but will share at the Leftover Party

CHAPTER 8

ALIVE WITH EXPECTATION

Advent

Christmas decorations seem to appear earlier every year, but instead of being Scrooge, let your spiritual emphasis begin early too. Long ago and continuing today, Christians did just that, designating the special season before Christmas as *Advent,* a word that means "coming." Advent is a time to prepare our hearts and anticipate the coming celebration.

During Advent we anticipate the joyful celebration of Christ's birth. We also acknowledge and reflect on Christ's presence in everyday life. Ironically, in this season of expectation we are often busy and distracted from spiritual things. We have gifts to buy or make, presents to wrap, cookies to bake, parties to attend, and family gatherings to plan. Most of us need help to stay focused on the spiritual, and that's what this chapter and a portion of chapter 10 offer. A meaningful Advent leads to a more meaningful Christmas.

COUNT THE DAYS

When we're preparing for something special, we naturally begin to think, "How much more time do I have to get things done?" When children wait anxiously for Christmas Day, they ask, "How many more days until Christmas?"

Advent calendars provide a festive way to count the days until Christmas, and many help focus little ones on the coming of the baby Jesus rather than the coming of Santa. Make your own Advent calendar or buy one at a card shop or

bookstore. Most commercial ones will begin with December 1 and have a twenty-four- or twenty-five-day observance. Advent actually begins on the fourth Sunday before Christmas Day (that's often in late November) and extends through Christmas Eve, so the number of days can vary from twenty-two to twenty-eight.

AN ADVENT CHAIN

An Advent chain accomplishes the same purpose as an Advent calendar: It helps mark the days until Christmas. To make a chain of twenty-five links, you will need twenty-four strips of paper, about seven inches long by one inch wide. On one side of each strip, write the date (December 1, December 2, and so on). On the other side (what will be the inside of the link), write out some verses from an easy-to-read translation or paraphrase of the story of Jesus' birth or use your own words. Make sure that your links tell the events leading up to Jesus' birth in sequence.

For example:

December 1

One day God sent his angel Gabriel to a young woman named Mary to tell her some wonderful news.

December 2

When Gabriel appeared to Mary, she was frightened. He told her not to be afraid, for God had chosen her above all women for a very special task.

December 3

Gabriel told Mary that she was going to have a baby, and the baby would be the Messiah, the Son of God.

Celebrate Advent and Christmas in a family way. The play on words is intentional. We're expecting! We're expecting Christmas and the retelling of the birth of Jesus. That's obvious, but that's not all.

Advent reminds us that we are all expectant people, people in waiting, people of promise. Our faith is built on God's promises fulfilled and yet to be fulfilled. We are by God's grace pregnant with new life and eternal hope.[1]

—The Schroeder Family, *Celebrate While We Wait*

Cut slots in each end on opposite sides of the strip. Place one slot within the other to form a link. Place a second strip into the first one and so on. Connect the twenty-four strips to make a chain. Hang it on your Christmas tree or near your dining table—someplace where it's easily accessible to the family. Each day, remove a link and read aloud the contents.

If you use slots in the links (rather than gluing or stapling the links together), you can use the chain year after year. On the other hand, you might want to make new chains so you can change the contents of the links. You could, for instance, print Bible verses that

- show what Jesus was like, what he said, and what he did when he was on earth

- reflect on the meaning of Jesus' coming at Bethlehem

- are prophecies fulfilled in Jesus' coming

- refer to Jesus' second coming

If you use an Advent chain with the story of Jesus' birth written line by line on the inside of the links, you can also use the links as a puzzle on Christmas Eve or Christmas Day. Put all the links on the table, with the content side faceup. Ask family members and guests to arrange the links in order of their occurrence.

Our family keeps an Advent calendar during December. Sometimes we hang homemade symbols of Christmas onto a tree, counting down the days. One of my favorites is carrying out our "24 ways to celebrate Advent." Each day we open an envelope on the tree and find a suggestion such as: "Write someone and express your gratitude, forgive an old hurt, tell someone you love him, or name your blessings."[2]
—Sue Monk Kidd, *Guideposts*

DECK THE HALLS

Advent calendars didn't work well at our house. The spiritual emphasis was minimal, and those fold-out windows got opened long before their due dates! Also, I was never very excited about having a countdown for Christmas. It only seemed to make my children think about how many days were left before they got to open their gifts. I did, however, want a day-to-day observance with some spiritual substance to it. So, with the help of a friend, I developed twenty-five devotional thoughts beginning with Jesus' birth and continuing through his resurrection. We made a corresponding felt symbol for each.

No sewing was involved. I made the symbols out of brightly colored felt scraps, and each day placed a felt symbol on a green felt tree. Since felt adheres to felt, no pins or glue are needed to hold the symbols in place. But you can make the same symbols out of paper and paste them on a paper tree. If you're really ambitious, you can make ornaments to hang on your Christmas tree.

I've included a summary of each devotional and its corresponding symbol below. (The complete devotional readings, the patterns for the symbols, and the instructions for making a felt tree wall hanging are available in my booklet *Celebrating the Life of Jesus.* For a copy, send $6 to me at 406 Edgewood Road, Union, MO 63084.)

Christmas is..."the beginning of the unfolding of God's plan of redemption, the opening scene of His Passion Play. To focus only on the Babe in the manger and the surrounding events, as miraculous as they are, is to lose sight of *who* that Baby was. He was not a sweet little baby boy; He was the omnipotent, victorious Savior of the universe. Only when we understand this can we begin to comprehend the truly incredible nature of what happened in Bethlehem."[3]

—Evelyn Christenson, *What Happens When We Pray for Our Families*

December 1: Birthday Candle

During December we will be getting ready to celebrate a special birthday. Let's put a birthday candle on our tree to remind us that this is the time of year we celebrate Jesus' birth.

December 2: Birthday Card

Each day until Christmas, we're going to talk about Jesus and then hang an appropriate ornament on our tree. These ornaments will be like birthday cards to Jesus.

December 3: Bible

The Bible can help us prepare our birthday cards. God's Word tells us about Jesus—what happened before he came, what he did during his life, what remarkable thing happened three days after his death, and what a difference his coming makes for you and me.

December 4: Flower

Old Testament prophets predicted the coming of Jesus. The prophet Isaiah, for instance, said that Jesus' coming would be as unusual as a rose blooming in the desert (Isaiah 35:1-2).

December 5: Clock

Jesus came in the fullness of time (Galatians 4:4): God had everything ready.

December 6: Manger

When the time was just right, Jesus was born in a stable in Bethlehem (Luke 2:1-7).

December 7: Shepherd's Crook

Angels appeared to nearby shepherds and told them about baby Jesus (Luke 2:8-20).

December 8: Star

The night Jesus was born, a bright star appeared in the sky. Some Wise Men were intrigued by it and followed it until they found Jesus (Matthew 2:1-12).

December 9: Temple

One of the things Jesus liked to do as a boy was to visit the temple (Luke 2:41-51). Jesus grew into a fine boy who pleased both God and those around him (Luke 2:52).

December 10: Dove

Before Jesus began his ministry, he was baptized. It was a wonderful event. The sky opened, a dove flew down to rest on Jesus, and God said, "This is my beloved Son, in whom I am well pleased" (Matthew 3:16-17).

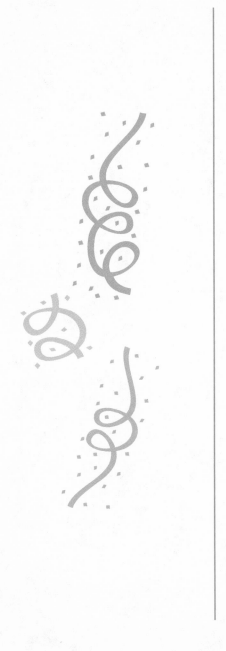

December 11: Goblet

People had never known anyone quite like Jesus. They first noticed how unusual he was when he turned water into wine at a wedding (John 2:1-11).

December 12: Fish

Jesus chose twelve special helpers to help him share the news of God's kingdom. He called them "fishers of men" (Mark 1:16-20, Luke 6:12-16).

December 13: Boat

Sometimes the crowds listening to Jesus would get so large and move in so near to him that he would have to get into a boat to preach (Mark 3:7-12). When he preached, Jesus often told things about himself. In the next few days, we're going to hear some of the things he said.

December 14: Lamp

Jesus said, "I am the light of the world" (John 1:4-9; 8:12; 9:5).

December 15: Door

Jesus said, "I am the door of the sheep" (John 10:7,9).

December 16: Lamb

Jesus said, "I am the good shepherd" (Luke 15:3-7; John 10:11,14).

December 17: Sheaf of Wheat

Jesus said, "I am the bread of life" (John 6:35).

December 18: Cluster of Grapes

Jesus wanted his followers to remember him always, so he asked them to participate in a simple meal of bread and wine. He compared his body to bread and said that his body was going to be broken. He compared his blood to the wine and said that his blood was going to be shed for the forgiveness of sin. Jesus was preparing his helpers for his death (Matthew 26:26-30; Mark 14:22-26; Luke 22:14-20). We already have wheat for bread on our tree, so today let's add grapes to represent the wine.

December 19: Crown of Thorns

Not everyone liked Jesus' preaching, and some of these people had him arrested. They accused him of wanting to be king and gave him a crown of thorns to wear (Matthew 27:27-31).

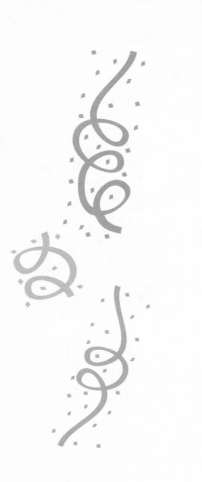

December 20: Cross

Jesus died on a big wooden cross (Matthew 27:31-33; John 19:16-18).

December 21: Butterfly

Jesus died and was buried, but he didn't stay in his grave. Like a butterfly emerging from a cocoon, he emerged from the tomb, alive again and victorious over death (1 Corinthians 15:3-8).

December 22: Triangle

Jesus eventually returned to heaven, but when he did he gave all believers his powerful Holy Spirit (John 14:15-17; Acts 2:1-12). The triangle with its three points reminds us of the three ways God appears to us: as the Father, as the Son, Jesus, and as the Holy Spirit.

December 23: Heart

The Holy Spirit can make anyone recognize Jesus as God's Son and our Savior, so why doesn't everyone believe in Jesus? Because we have to open our hearts. Jesus knocks on the door of our hearts, wanting to come in (Revelation 3:20), but not everyone welcomes him.

December 24: Gift

When we open ourselves to Jesus and name him as our Savior and Lord, he gives himself to us, taking the punishment for our sin, welcoming us into God's family 1 John 3:1), and enabling us to enjoy eternal life with him and our heavenly Father. God saw that we needed someone like Jesus and gave him to us (John 3:16). Jesus is God's gift to us (2 Corinthians 9:15).

December 25: Crown

Jesus was the king the Wise Men were searching for, but his kingdom differs from other kingdoms (John 18:36). The kingdom of Jesus, the kingdom of God, is not based on force, guns, money, or power. His kingdom is in our hearts and is based on love. Let's put a crown on our tree to recognize Jesus' birthday and to acknowledge that he is on the throne of our hearts.

Beginning December 1 and continuing each day through Christmas Day, one of our sons placed a symbol on the tree while my husband or I explained its significance. Eventually the boys took turns explaining each symbol themselves. We repeated this activity every year until our youngest was a junior in high school.

MAKE A JESSE TREE

Named from a prophecy about Jesus in Isaiah 11:1: "A shoot will come up from the stump of Jesse; from his roots a Branch will bear fruit" (NIV), this tree is a reminder of our glorious heritage, firmly rooted in Christ. Use ornaments associated with Old Testament events from creation to the birth of Jesus: a rainbow for Noah's ark, a scroll of paper representing the Law, a tiny lamp for the Word of God.[4]

—Jan Dargatz, *Virtue*

To make the kind of felt symbols we used in our Advent devotionals, think one-dimensional and draw a simple outline of the object on paper to make a pattern. Cut out the pattern, place it on a piece of felt, and then cut around it. Most of these symbols will be easily identifiable from the felt figure. Others may need some additional details. For example, a black piece of felt cut in the shape of an open book may not look like a Bible, the symbol for December 3. To make it look more like an open Bible, glue a smaller piece of white felt on the top of the black piece and add a piece of red thread down the middle as a bookmark.

To make a felt tree, draw half a Christmas tree along the folded edge of a large piece of paper. Cut along the lines of your drawing, unfold the paper, and you'll have a pattern. Pin your pattern to a piece of green felt. Cut the felt along the edges of the pattern, unpin the pattern piece, and pin your felt tree on the wall near your dining table.

We glued our felt tree to a square piece of burlap and used it as a wall hanging (which made it easy to keep from year to year). We fringed the burlap on three sides and folded the fourth side under to make a pocket for a dowel. A decorative cord connected to the ends of the dowel made the finished piece easy to hang.

We placed our wall hanging by our kitchen table, and every morning during December the boys took turns reading the devotional thoughts and placing the symbols on our felt Christmas tree. Another family used the readings at bedtime. They sang a carol or two by candlelight, read the devotional, placed the symbol on the tree, and ended with prayer.

GIVE DAILY GIFTS

Wrap twenty-five small "mystery" packages, each containing one of the items listed below together with the accompanying explanation and Bible reference. On the outside of each package, write the date it is to be opened. Place the packages in a basket near the Christmas tree and open one each night. Be aware that excited little hands may sort through the basket when your back is turned. If that happens, bring the basket out each evening and let the kids find the gift to be opened that day. Have a Bible handy for reading the suggested passage.

December 1: A Quarter

A quarter! That equals twenty-five cents. But twenty-five is also the number of days until Christmas, when God gave us his best present. Jesus told about one woman's gift and the way she gave it. (Read Mark 12:41-44.)

December 2: A Piece of Grape Gum

Grapes make jelly and juice, raisins, and wine.
But Jesus didn't need grapes to perform his first
miracle. (Read John 2:1-11.)

December 3: A Smiley Face Sticker

Here's a smile! A smile usually expresses happiness.
Jesus gave us many instructions to keep us happy.
(Read Matthew 5:1-12.)

December 4: A Few Fish Crackers

If you were surprised to find these fish, wait till
you read the story today! Others were surprised to
find fish too. (Read Luke 5:4-10.)

December 5: One Birthday Candle

As you know, we're getting ready to celebrate Jesus'
birthday. However, Jesus talked about something
else that is related to this candle. He talked about
light. (Read Matthew 5:14-16.)

December 6: A Small Jingle Bell

You could make some noise with this, but it would
not have bothered a certain man—until he met
Jesus. (Read Mark 7:31-37.)

December 7: Two Small Pieces of Candy

These would not go very far if you were really hungry. But Jesus could make much out of little. He sure knew how to multiply! (Read Matthew 14:13-21.)

December 8: Two Cotton Balls

These cotton balls would be helpful in a thunderstorm, wouldn't they? We could use them for earplugs to muffle the loud noises that thunder makes. But we know someone who doesn't need cotton to block the thunder's noise. He simply makes the thunder stop. Jesus can control the weather. (Read Matthew 8:23-27.)

December 9: A Piece of Road Map

People needing to use the other parts of this map are in trouble. Don't you get lost today! (Read John 14:1-6.)

December 10: A Small Piece of Soap

Do you like to wash your hands and face? Behind your ears? Washing turned out to be a happy time for many who met Jesus. (Read John 9:1-7.)

December 11: A Few Candy Hearts

Hearts speak of love, don't they? Jesus spoke some commands about love. (Read Matthew 22:37-40.)

December 12: A Tiny Cross or a Pin-On Button with a Cross Printed on It

We use the cross as a symbol that points to Jesus. Do you know why it reminds us of Jesus? (Read Philippians 2:1-11.)

December 13: A Small Packet of Salt

Jesus said that we were to be like salt in this world. He also gave us some advice. (Read Matthew 5:13 and Colossians 4:6.)

December 14: A Small Bag of Sand

Sand reminds us that Jesus knew something about architecture, about buildings—and about building lives. (See his instructions in Matthew 7:24-29.)

December 15: A Small Artificial Flower

Flowers are pretty, aren't they? Jesus used flowers to teach us a reassuring lesson. (Read Matthew 6:28-34.)

December 16: A Little Box of Raisins

Many children are given raisins instead of candy for a snack. That's because they are a healthy and delicious fruit. Jesus told us how we can produce good fruit. (Read John 15:1-5.)

December 17: A Few Flower Seeds

Jesus told a story about a man who planted some seeds. Then he explained the story, revealing its deeper meaning. (Read Matthew 13:3-8, 18-23.)

December 18: A Printed Christmas Carol

Christmas is just a week away, and here is an appropriate song. Let's sing it loudly! (After the song read Psalm 100.)

December 19: A Little Stone

Can you change this stone into a piece of bread? Do you think Jesus could? Satan asked Jesus to do just that. Do you know how he answered? (Read Matthew 4:1-4.)

December 20: A Piece of Crumpled Aluminum Foil

Try to smooth out this piece of aluminum foil and use it as a mirror. It's hard to see your reflection,

HELP OTHERS CELEBRATE WHILE THEY WAIT

Prepare one of the advent observances described in this chapter (the chain, the tree with its felt symbols, or the basket of mysterious packages) and give it to another family. The gift will be very well received, and it will add meaning to another family's Advent season.

- One woman made wall hangings with felt symbols for families in a low-income housing area near her church. She printed devotional booklets to go along with them.

- A teenager made paper chains and delivered them to her baby-sitting clients.

- One woman made a tree out of paper, cut symbols from old Christmas cards and magazines, and then sent this Advent celebration kit to a man in prison. With it she sent her prayers: "Dear Lord, let John know that this family is with him in spirit. Let this tree carry the joy and peace and the good will that Christmas holds for all of us."[5]

isn't it? Many circumstances of our lives and in the world around us are hard to understand, but someday everything will be clear. (Read 1 Corinthians 13:12.)

December 21: One Mustard Seed (placed between two pieces of clear contact paper)

The mustard seed is very small. But when it sprouts, it grows into a large plant. See what Jesus said about it. (Read Matthew 17:20.)

December 22: A Tiny Plastic Dove

We've learned that the cross represents Jesus, but do you know who the dove stands for? (Read Matthew 3:13-17.)

December 23: A Swatch of Wool Fabric

The threads of this fabric came from the wool of a sheep. Jesus called himself the Good Shepherd. Do you know who his sheep are? (Read John 10:7-18.)

December 24: One Blue Marble

Do you know what is sometimes called the "Big Blue Marble"? The world. God made the world for us. What does God continue doing to the world? And who is the world? (Read John 3:16.)

December 25: A Small Photograph of a Baby

Isn't this baby cute? When he was born, he made a whole family happy. Jesus was born as a baby too. He came to make the whole world happy. (Read Luke 2:1-20.)[6]

Christmas decorations go up far in advance of the holiday, so your spiritual emphasis can begin early too. The joyful sights and sounds of Christmas provide just the right atmosphere for reflecting on the meaning of the season. Every day in some small way you can focus on Jesus with wondrous expectation.

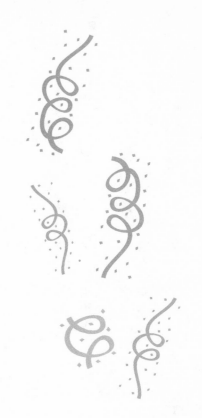

CHAPTER 9

"LIGHT OF THE WORLD"

Christmas by Candlelight

Jesus, the Light of the World, is born! The Savior—promised by the prophets long ago, heralded by the angels, welcomed by the shepherds, and worshiped by the Wise Men—has come! More than two thousand years later his light still shines in the darkness; the darkness has not overcome it! With so many lights twinkling around us at Christmastime, we have many opportunities to celebrate this aspect of Christ's nature.

Candles are an especially good way to celebrate Jesus as the Light of the World because children and adults relate candles to celebrations. Candles do make an occasion special, and their glow fascinates children. So here are some ideas for how to use candles during the Christmas season to point to Christ. When you connect candlelight to Jesus, your Christmas will glow with meaning.

ADVENT WREATHS

Fashioned from evergreen boughs, an Advent wreath may be purchased in floral shops, ordered through gift catalogs, or made at home. Traditionally, the wreath holds four candles, three purple and one rose (pink). The rose candle stands for joy; the purple candles represent penitence.[1] Sometimes, a white candle is placed in the center of the wreath. It is called the Christ candle; the color white reflects his purity. He is "a lamb without blemish" (1 Peter 1:19).

Light one purple candle on the fourth Sunday before Christmas (the first Sunday of Advent). On the next Sunday, light the same purple candle and another purple candle. On the third Sunday, light the two candles you've already lighted and the rose one. On the fourth Sunday, light all the candles in the wreath. If you've included the fifth candle, light it on Christmas Eve or Christmas Day.

Bible reading, prayer, and a song accompany the weekly candle lighting. Each candle can be used as a symbol beyond penitence and joy. Your church may be able to recommend a particular combination of Bible reading, prayers, and symbolism. If not, here's a sample of what your observance might look like if you designate the four candles of the Advent wreath as promise, light, love, and hope.[2]

Candle 1: The Promise of Jesus' Coming

Reflection: Long before Jesus was born, God promised it would be (Isaiah 7:14; 9:6; Micah 5:2).

Prayer: Thank you, God, that you kept your promise to send your Son to save us.

Song: "O Come, O Come, Emmanuel"

Candle 2: The Light of the World

Reflection: The candle of light reminds us of the star the Wise Men followed (Matthew 2:1-2,9-10).

Jesus said to the people, "I am the Light of the world. So if you follow me, you won't be stumbling through the darkness, for living light will flood your path."

John 8:12, TLB

Prayer: Dear Father, you gave the Wise Men a light to show them the way. Thank you for sending Jesus as Light of the World, to light our path and to guide us.

Song: "We Three Kings of Orient Are"

Candle 3: We Love Him Because He First Loved Us

Reflection: The candle of love reminds us that God wants us to love him (1 John 4:16-19).

Prayer: Dear Lord, we know that you love us, and we want to love you. Help us to show our love for you every day.

Song: "O Come, All Ye Faithful"

Candle 4: The Hope of His Soon Return

Reflection: The candle of hope reminds us that God gave us a gift of hope—life forever with him (Titus 2:13).

Prayer: Dear God, thank you for the wonderful hope that is ours because we know Jesus will come again.

Song: "Joy to the World"

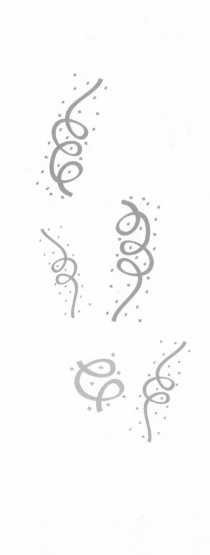

Add a dramatic touch to the weekly candle-lighting ceremony by quoting John 8:12: "Then spake Jesus again unto them, saying, I am the light of the world: he that followeth me shall not walk in

MAKE YOUR OWN ADVENT WREATH

To make an Advent wreath, buy a Styrofoam ring at a craft store. This will be your base. Make small holes in the ring so the candles will fit snugly and firmly. Cut your greens into six- to eight-inch lengths. Use wire to attach greens to the base: Wrap wire around the wreath, catching bunches of greens as you go. Lay greens in the same direction all the way around so that the top of each new bunch covers the stems of the last bunch that you attached to the base. You can leave the wreath plain or add ribbons, glitter, gold and silver decorations, or pine cones.

darkness, but shall have the light of life." Arrange ahead of time for someone to respond to the verse with a question, "Why do we light one candle?" A parent responds by saying, "The candle reminds us of the promise of Jesus' coming." The second week, after the quoting of John 8:12, another person asks, "Why do we light two candles?" and so on.

GET THE CHILDREN INVOLVED

- Advent candles can be good teaching tools for young children. Say "As we light the third candle, who can tell me what the first candle stands for? What does the second candle stand for?" Each week, use the candles to review the story of Jesus' birth.

- Each week, you might assign a different child the responsibility of having the candles, the Bible, or the songbooks ready for your candlelight service.

- Have the children make an Advent booklet for each family member. Each booklet could contain the songs, the Bible passages, and the prayer thoughts. Use a sturdy paper for the binder and let the children decorate it with pictures from old Christmas cards. This could be the children's Christmas gift to the family—and everything will be ready for years to come.

CHANGE THE SYMBOLISM

Most families enjoy the weekly candle-lighting ceremony so much that they want to repeat it year after year. However, the points of reflection may become so familiar to participants that the ceremony loses its meaning. As your children grow older, or if you are celebrating with adults, you may want to employ different symbolism and accompanying scriptures. Here are three alternatives:

1. The "I AM" statements Jesus made about himself can be assigned to the candles on an Advent wreath. Choose four or five of the following six statements.

   Candle 1: "I am the light of the world" (John 8:12; 9:5).

   Candle 2: "I am the bread of life" (John 6:35).

   Candle 3: "I am the door" (John 10:7,9).

   Candle 4: "I am the good shepherd" (John 10:11,14).

   Candle 5: "I am the resurrection, and the life" (John 11:25).

   Candle 6: "I am the vine, ye are the branches" (John 15:5).

2. Center your weekly candle-lighting ceremony on some of the different times Jesus comes to the believer, his "advents."[4] Advent means "coming" or "arrival."

OPENING NIGHT JITTERS

On the first night of Advent, the first child said, "It's my turn to light the candle." The second child said, "You did it first last year; it's my turn!" The third child said, "Daddy, you promised me last year that I could do it first this year."

Father said, "Look, there's only one candle..."

First child responded, "Yes, and it's my turn!" and the arguing continued.

Finally Father had the inspiration of having one child strike the match, one child light the candle, and one child blow it out. He was lucky the baby was too young to speak up![3]

Pink candle: As this candle is lighted, a child says, "Jesus came in the flesh when he was born at Bethlehem."

Prayer: Thank you, Jesus, for coming in the flesh and giving up heaven to reveal God to us.

Red candle: As the second candle is lighted, a child says, "Jesus came to die on the cross for our sins. Jesus comes to wash us with his blood."

Prayer: Thank you, Jesus, for your saving blood and for shedding it for us.

Blue candle: As this candle is lighted, a child says, "Jesus comes to be with us day by day. His Spirit reveals himself to us."

Prayer: Thank you, Jesus, for being with us through the presence of the Holy Spirit.

White candle: As this candle is lighted, a child says, "Jesus will come to earth again one day."

Prayer: Thank you, Jesus, that one day you will return to earth and defeat Satan once and for all.

3. Make each candle lighting an opportunity to consider the effect of Christ's birth on our daily lives.[5] Ask family members to thoughtfully reflect on what they can learn from the scripture being read. Invite but don't force people to share their ideas.

First week: Light a candle and consider what characteristics will mark a person who is watching and ready for Christ's Second Coming.

Read: Isaiah 2:1-5; Matthew 24:37-44; Romans 13:8-14

Second week: Light two candles and consider the reign of Christ in your lives—is he Lord of every area?

Read: Isaiah 11:1-10; Romans 15:4-13; Matthew 3:1-12

Third week: Light three candles and consider the joy we have when we trust Jesus as our Savior.

Read: Isaiah 12:1-6; 35:1-10; Matthew 11:2-11; Philippians 2:9-11; 4:4

Fourth week: Light four candles and consider the significance of the names of Jesus.

Read: Isaiah 7:14; 9:6; Matthew 1:18-25

SAFELY CELEBRATE "THE LIGHT"

Although they are beautiful symbols, candles can be dangerous. Be sure to keep all lighted candles away from flammable materials. Keep matches and lighters out of the reach of children. Do not leave children alone in a room where candles are burning. Keep lighted candles away from small fingers, but do let the children blow them out when the ceremony is completed. That's part of the fun!

CANDLES OF JOY

When a friend first told me about the Advent wreath, I liked the idea, but then I didn't have the money to buy a wreath or the time to make one. But I did find a five-pronged candleholder for two dollars. I bought it, took it home, and placed some greenery in, around, and through it. My sons and I put five long red tapers into the candleholders. We wanted red because we associated that color with joy, and our emphasis was celebration.

Our family switched the weekly candle-lighting ceremony from Sundays to Saturday nights because of the amount of time we spent in church on Sundays. (You can light your Advent candles any day of the week when everyone is present.)

We made the Saturday evening meal special by using a tablecloth and our best dishes, and we ate at the dining-room table together. We didn't change what we ate, just where and how we ate. The extra attention to the meal indicated to the children that this was an important occasion.

While I was in the kitchen putting the finishing touches on the food, my husband gathered the boys at the table. They sang Christmas carols as I put the food on the table. When I was seated, Bob or one of the boys read the Scripture passage. We lit the appropriate candles, Bob prayed, and we enjoyed the candlelight while we ate our meal. This became a "must do" activity for us for several years. Here's what our observance included:

Candle 1:	**The Promise of Jesus' Coming**
Bible reading:	Isaiah 9:6-7
Prayer thought:	Help us prepare for the celebration of the coming of Jesus. Prepare our hearts, that we may be filled with wonder and receive him with praise.
Song:	"O Come, O Come, Emmanuel"

Christmas candles can claim a high antiquity. The Jews, at their yearly 'Feast of lights'...set up many...in honor of the feast.... It was usual all through the Middle Ages to set up on Christmas Eve, both in church and hall, one very large candle in remembrance of the Star of Bethlehem; or perhaps in remembrance of the words of Simeon, who spoke of the Holy Child as 'A Light to lighten the Gentiles.'"[6]
—T. G. Crippen, *Christmas and Christmas Lore*

Candle 2: **Mary and Joseph's Trip to Bethlehem**

Bible reading: Luke 2:1-5

Prayer thought: Just as Mary and Joseph went expectantly to Bethlehem, we expectantly prepare for the coming of Christ. Help us in our preparation to be ready to receive him.

Song: "O Come, All Ye Faithful"

Candle 3: **No Room in the Inn**

Bible reading: Luke 2:6-7

Prayer thought: Come into our home this Christmas. We have room for you.

Song: "O Little Town of Bethlehem"

Candle 4: **The Shepherds Receive the Message from the Angels**

Bible reading: Luke 2:8-15

Prayer thought: Let the glory of the Lord shine upon us and give us peace and gladness. Help us to share our joy with others.

Song: "Hark! The Herald Angels Sing"

Candle 5: **Wise Men Visit the Newborn King**

Bible reading: Matthew 2:1-2,9-11

Prayer thought:	We thank you, God, for the reminder of giving through the gifts of the Wise Men. Thank you for the gift of your Son, Jesus. Thank you for the gifts we receive this Christmas and for the chance to give to others.
Song:	"Joy to the World"

If you want to adapt our five-candle ceremonies to work for four candles, you might combine candles 2 and 3:

Candle:	**Mary and Joseph's Trip to Bethlehem**
Bible reading:	Luke 2:1-7
Prayer thought:	There was no room for Mary and Joseph in the busy inns of Bethlehem. When we welcome Jesus, may we not be like the innkeepers who turned away Mary and Joseph. Instead, help us make room for Jesus in our lives and in our hearts.
Song:	"O Little Town of Bethlehem"

A weekly candle-lighting ceremony—whether traditional or personalized—is an effective tool for celebrating Jesus as the Light of the World, but it is not the only way.

HIGHLIGHTING JESUS

Our Christmas celebration begins about a month before Christmas through our adaptation of the Advent Wreath. At dessert time on the first Sunday of Advent the youngest child lights the first candle, I read Scripture, and the child shares a word about his Christian experience. We pray, and he snuffs out the candle.

The next week the next child takes the responsibility. The theme for sharing may be "How I came to Christ," or "What Christ has come to mean to me this year," or "How I have grown in my understanding of following Christ this year."[7]

—Howard A. Whaley, *Moody*

CELEBRATE "THE LIGHT" EVERYDAY

A Missouri family created a log of light to celebrate "The Light" during Advent. They selected a log that was six feet long and about four inches in diameter, then planed one side so that it would sit securely on the fireplace mantel. Along the top of the log, they drilled twenty-eight holes in a row, equally spaced for the number of days in the season of Advent.[8] (As explained in chapter 8, Advent begins on the fourth Sunday before Christmas and ends on December 24. The season varies in length from twenty-two to twenty-eight days. Twenty-eight holes assures always having enough.)

Here's how to make this activity a part of your celebration:

Place a candle in each hole. In order to provide approximately twenty minutes of candlelight each day, use a good quality candle that is fifteen to eighteen inches tall. Slow-burning ones are available.

Starting the first day of Advent, light the candle at one end of the log. On the second day of Advent, light the first candle plus a second one at the opposite end. Each day light another candle, alternating ends, until Christmas Eve.

The last lighted candle forms the apex of a pyramid of light. Both the warmth and the magnitude of the light increases as the number of lighted candles increases—a symbolic reminder of how we can increase the illuminating power of Jesus by sharing him with others.

You might want to read a Bible verse or have a short devotional with each day's candle lighting. Daily December devotional thoughts are included in chapter 8 on pages 83-89.

CELEBRATE "THE LIGHT" WHEN EXCHANGING GIFTS

In *Parties with a Purpose,* Marlene D. LeFever suggests a candle ceremony that would work at gift exchanges for families or church groups.[9] After the gifts are opened, give each person a candle. Have an adult light a large candle and place it in the middle of the room, then explain that the large candle symbolizes Christ, the Light of the world, and that each smaller candle represents the person holding it. Then invite each person to take his or her candle to the large one and light it, explaining that this symbolizes a desire for Christ to shine through our lives and for us to share the light of Jesus with those who are in darkness.

After the candles are burning, sing together the Doxology or "I Have Decided to Follow Jesus." This simple ceremony takes only a few minutes, yet it says so much at a time when the reason for celebrating may easily be overlooked.

CELEBRATE "THE LIGHT" WITH ANGEL CHIMES

Christmas gift shops and discount stores often sell angel chimes. These light gold-colored metal chimes consist of four angels hanging above four candles. When the candles are lighted, the angels go round and round, like a small merry-go-round. As the angels move, little pins on the bottoms of the angels expand and hit the two chimes, making a lovely sound.

When young children see the angels turning for the first time, they are bound to ask, "How do they do that?" This is a wonderful opportunity to teach them about the Holy Spirit.

LET THE LIGHT SHINE

To us, celebrating Christmas openly is a privilege after living in a Communist country where Christmas is replaced by a winter festival.

In Romania, lighted candles were an expression of Christ because we could have no detailed or specific representations. Candles were the insistent expression of the true meaning of Christmas—Christ is the Light of the World. People lighted candles in windows and Christians sent cards illustrated with a burning candle.

This is a tradition we brought with us to the States. Candles burn throughout our house, symbolizing our freedom in Christ.[10]

—Mercedes Andrei, *Virtue*

"Grandpa, what makes the angels go round and round?"

"Do you see a motor?" responds Grandpa.

"No," the children answer.

"Did we put any batteries in it?"

"No. Come on, Grandpa, tell us what makes it work."

"Your wanting to know how it works makes me think of Nicode-

mus. He couldn't understand how God's Spirit works. Jesus explained to him that the Spirit is like the wind. We can feel the wind, we can hear the wind, and we can see its effect, but we can't see it or touch it. The Holy Spirit is the same way. We can't see him, but we know he is with us because he helps us know Jesus as a friend."

The angel chimes can help explain to children something of the mystery of the Holy Spirit, who helps all of us experience Jesus as the Light of the world.

Whether you choose to use candles one time, four times, or every day during the Christmas season, they will greatly enrich your celebration. Not only do candles create a special atmosphere and make your home attractive, but most important, they remind us that Jesus is the Light of the World. With candles, we can celebrate the one who brought us "out of darkness into his marvellous light" (1 Peter 2:9).

TIN-CAN LANTERN

To emphasize Jesus as the Light of the World, make tin-can lanterns to hold thick long-burning candles. The trick of this holiday craft is to put water in a tin can and freeze it before pounding holes in it with a hammer and nail to make a lantern. Experiment with different patterns of nail holes to make Christian symbols such as crosses, angels, and stars. These lanterns work well sitting outside on the front porch or lining the front walkway.

CHAPTER 10

STOP, LOOK, AND LISTEN AT THE MANGER

Christmas

On impulse one year, I placed an extra character in my Nativity scene. As I nestled Mary, Joseph, the shepherds, and the Wise Men amid evergreens on the fireplace mantel, I added another woodcarving, that of an African woman, a gift from a missionary. The original Nativity figures all came from the same brown wood and were carved in proportion to each other. This late arrival, however, was taller than the Wise Men and carved out of ebony. As I hummed "Joy to the World," I thought about what I would say when someone asked me why the woman was there. *I know. I'll tell them, "The birth of Jesus is significant because he came for every person—rich and poor, black and white, young and old, educated and uneducated, male and female."*

But I never got a chance to give my little speech. No one asked about the woman! Perhaps they were thinking, *Brenda certainly has weird decorating tastes!* I suspect, though, that most people never mentioned her because they never saw her. It never occurred to them that they might find anything different in the Nativity scene, so they never looked closely at it.

Like those visitors to my house during that Advent season, we, too, tend to expect the same old same old. Because we do the same things year after year, it's easy to walk past the very heart of

Christmas without even realizing it. But if we want to focus on meaning, we may have to stop, look, and listen. What better place to begin than at the manger?

READING THE BIBLICAL STORY

In our culture the line between truth and fantasy seems to be blurred at Christmastime. Children lump Jesus, Mary, and Joseph right in with Rudolph, the Grinch, Frosty the Snowman, and Santa's elves. Even for many adults, Bible stories seem to have taken place in the Land of Make-Believe, yet the events of the Christmas story took place in history. The manger reminds us that Jesus' birth was a real event, not a myth or a fairy tale. That rough-hewn feeding trough reminds us that God took on human form at a point in time. "The Word became flesh and made his dwelling among us" (John 1:14, NIV).

To keep this truth central to your celebration, read your family the story of Jesus' birth. You might want to read the whole story on Christmas Eve or Christmas Day, or you might want to stretch the story out, reading a different portion each day for several days. You'll find the biblical account in Luke 1:26-56 and 2:1-40 and Matthew 1:18–2:23. Luke describes the angel's appearance to Mary, Mary's visit to her cousin Elizabeth, Mary and Joseph's journey to Bethlehem, the birth of Jesus in the stable, and the shepherds' visit. Matthew tells about the Wise Men, Herod's cold-blooded slaughter of all the male babies two years of age or younger, and the escape of Mary, Joseph, and their baby into Egypt.

With Young Children

- Read the Christmas story in short sections over a period of several days or tell the story in your own words with the Bible open on your lap. Place the appropriate figures in your Nativity scene as the story is told. One family I know thought of a way to emphasize the Wise Men's long journey to worship the Messiah: They put the figures of the Wise Men at one end of the house and moved them slowly toward Bethlehem.

- After you have told the Christmas story using the figures, leave the crèche out for the children to play with. They will reenact the story of Jesus' birth again and again once they have learned it, so be sure to select an inexpensive Nativity scene made of durable materials. Expensive ceramic manger scenes are nice to look at, but they do little to enhance the meaning of Christmas if a child is forbidden to touch them. Saying "No, no. You mustn't touch baby Jesus" doesn't seem to fit the character of the one who said, "Suffer the little children to come unto me, and forbid them not" (Mark 10:14).

- Reinforce the Bible's account of Jesus' birth by singing carols such as "O Little Town of Bethlehem" and "Away in a Manger" and by teaching your kids this simple finger play about Mary and Jesus:

Let us never rise so high that we do not remain by the manger.

Martin Luther

THE WHOLE STORY OF JESUS' BIRTH

The Christmas story is often read aloud from Luke 2. For one continuous story, put Matthew's account together with Luke's account. Start with Luke 1:26. When you get to verse 56, go to Matthew 1:18. Read to verse 25, then return to Luke 2:1 and read to verse 38. Finally, turn back to Matthew and read all of chapter 2.

Here's Baby Jesus.

    (Hold up an index finger.)

Let's put him to bed.

    (Place finger in palm of other hand.)

And cover him up.

    (Four fingers close over index finger.)

All but his head.

    (Tip of finger extends out.)

And if he should cry,

    (Hold up index finger.)

We'll put him right here.

    (Place index finger on shoulder.)

And pretend that we're Mary

Who loved Jesus so dear.

    (Pat back of hand.)[1]

With Older Children

- Ask them to read the Bible story to you from a modern, easy-to-read version of the Bible such as *Today's English Version, The Living Bible,* or *The Message.*

- Wrap each figure from your Nativity scene in tissue paper. Tape a Scripture reference on the front of each package and put all the pieces in a basket. On Christmas Eve ask each child to pick a package, read the scripture, unwrap the figure, and place it in the crèche.

- Print portions of the Bible's account of Jesus' birth on pieces of paper. Give a different piece to each family member and ask each person to read his or her portions aloud. Then see if they can line themselves up in the order that the events occurred, according to their Scripture portion. Scripture portions in order of occurrence:

  1. Angel Announces Jesus' Birth to Mary (Luke 1:26-38)
  2. Mary Shares the News (Luke 1:39-45)
  3. Mary's Song of Praise (Luke 1:46-56)
  4. Joseph Learns About Jesus' Coming Birth (Matthew 1:18-25)
  5. The Birth of Jesus (Luke 2:1-7)
  6. The Shepherds and the Angels (Luke 2:8-20)

DID JESUS GET CHIGGERS?

I started using a crèche with movable figures when my older sons were preschoolers. I liked the results so much that I couldn't wait to do the same thing when our third child, Ben, was born, but in my eagerness I introduced it before he was ready. At twenty months, Ben found great delight in repeatedly sweeping the whole scene off onto the floor. Still, I was committed to finding some way to help Ben grasp the meaning of the manger. I asked my husband, Bob, to construct a manger from some weathered boards. I took a baby doll, wrapped it in "swaddling clothes," and laid it in the manger.

When Ben saw the manger for the first time, he reached for the doll, picked it up, then cuddled and patted it. When he did that, I said, "Jesus loves Ben." Many times during the days before Christmas, Ben picked up the baby doll and cuddled it. And each time I affirmed God's love for him.

Our family used the manger for several years. When we took it out of the storage shed each year, Ben always had questions: "Did Jesus grow up? What was he like? Where is he now?"

One year, as we brushed the bugs and cobwebs off the manger before taking it into the house, Ben asked, "Did Jesus get chiggers?" I could almost hear what Ben was thinking: How can you lay a baby in a feeding trough? Won't bugs get on him? Ben had grasped the reality of Jesus' birth: "The Word was made flesh, and dwelt among us" (John 1:14).

7. Jesus Is Named and Presented at the Temple (Luke 2:21-38)

8. The Wise Men Want to See Jesus (Matthew 2:1-12)

If you have fewer than eight people, you can either combine some of these passages or eliminate the first four and the seventh scripture portions. Also, if some of these are too long, you can divide them up and give them new titles. For example, "The Shepherds and the Angels" could be divided in two so that you have:

The Praise of the Angels (Luke 2:8-14)

The Shepherds' Excitement (Luke 2:15-20)

REENACTING THE STORY

Saint Francis of Assisi is credited with being the first person to stage a Nativity scene and reenact the story of Jesus' birth. He wanted to celebrate the incarnation in a special way that would help people remember the Christ child and how he was born. In his reenactment, Saint Francis used real people, a real manger, a real ox and ass, and real shepherds. Many churches repeat this time-honored tradition. You can do the same in your own home.

- When it's just family, let the children act out the parts. Not enough children for all the characters? No problem. Act out just a portion of the story or invite other children to join you.

HELPING KIDS CONNECT WITH THE STORY

Strengthen the impact of the Bible reading by using your imagination to make up stories about each person mentioned. Either let family members choose the characters they want to write about or put the names of Mary, Joseph, a shepherd, a Wise Man, and the innkeeper on slips of paper and have each family member draw one. Ask them to tell how the character was affected by Jesus' birth. The stories can be funny or serious. Read them aloud around the Christmas tree on Christmas Eve, then save them to read when your kids are older.

- When guests come over, ask the children to perform the story of Jesus' birth for the adults or have the adults perform for the children. Give actors some verbal instructions about what scenes to include and provide some costume material (old draperies, some bath towels, bathrobes, etc.). Then give their imaginations free rein. Don't worry about having the actors memorize their parts. Let everyone speak their own thoughts in their own way. That's when the story becomes real!

The Giving Manger

The manger is rarely a focal point of our Christmas decorations, yet its very presence can remind us of the reality of Jesus' birth and of his true nature as God made flesh.

- Fill a manger with inexpensive gifts that you have purchased throughout the year, and give them to your holiday visitors as they leave your home.[2]

- Bake small loaves of bread, wrap them in Saran Wrap, and place them in a manger to give to your guests. This is less expensive than purchasing gifts and has the added benefit of symbolism. The loaves point to Jesus, who is the Bread of Life (John 6:35, 48). You can explain this symbolism to your visitors when you hand them a loaf of bread from a real manger.

WHY THE MANGER IS IMPORTANT

In the first few hundred years of Christianity, the celebration of Jesus' birth was not emphasized. Heresies developed. Some people believed that Jesus was born a man and became the Son of God only at his baptism. Others said that Jesus was not really man at all, but only a phantom who appeared to be man. How better to counter these heresies than to celebrate the birth of Jesus as a flesh-and-blood baby, lying in a manger at Bethlehem?

- Small candles in a variety of shapes and colors also make appropriate manger gifts. Wrap each candle in a square of cellophane and tie it with ribbon. Attach a small card reading "Jesus is the Light of the world" (John 8:12; 9:5). Place the wrapped candles in the manger, ready to hand to guests as they leave.

- Fill the manger with Scripture. Print verses on sturdy white paper, roll them into little scrolls, and tie them with bright red bows. You could also order Scripture passages and other Bible-related products. The American Bible Society offers attractive, easy-to-read seasonal Bible passages as well as many inexpensive items for all ages that would work well in your giving manger. To request a catalog, contact the American Bible Society at P.O. Box 7251, Berlin, CT 06037, or visit their Web site at www.americanbible.org.

- Whatever gifts you choose for your manger, as you hand one to your visitors, say "I give this to you in the name of Jesus" or "I give this to you in the name of the one who has given so much to me."

An Acts-of-Kindness Manger

An old issue of *Better Homes and Gardens* tells of a Kentucky family who displays two baskets in their living room during the four weeks leading up to Christmas. One basket contains a bundle of straw, the other a figure of baby Jesus. Every time one of the family members treats another with special kindness, the recipient of the kind act transfers a small bit of straw to the basket where baby Jesus lies. The idea is that by the time Christmas Day comes, acts of kindness will have made the baby's bed soft with straw. Then early Christmas morning, the family comes downstairs together, softly singing "Happy Birthday" to Jesus.[3]

If you don't have room for two mangers, you can make a small

DOUBLE THE MEANING

If you have evergreens in your yard, fill your "giving manger" with ribbon-tied bunches of fresh greenery to give away. Your guests will appreciate receiving the greenery to use in decorating their own homes, and you will add to the significance of the manger: Traditional greenery such as pine, spruce, holly, and fir have long symbolized life because they remain green and vibrantly alive all year round. Evergreens can remind believers that, because of Christ's death on the cross, we have everlasting life.

CONSTRUCTING A MANGER

If you want a manger for decorative purposes, buy a long board, 1 x 12 x 87 inches. Cut the board in two pieces, one 54 inches long and the other one 33 inches long. Cut the 54-inch piece in half; this will give you the two sides (12 x 27 inches each) for the manger.

Cut the other piece into four long pieces of equal width (approximately 2-3/4 inches wide by 33 inches long). The four pieces will form the legs and support for the manger. Saw off ends of the four pieces at 45-degree angles, so when the legs are standing they will be flat on the floor and flat at the top. Use two for one end of the manger and two for the other end. Cross them at a point about 17 to 19 inches above the floor. The result will be two Xs. At the point where they cross, nail or screw the two pieces together.

In the heart of the X, place the 27-inch boards, one on each side of the top of the X. Nail the boards to the sides of the Xs. Attach a hook and eye fastener to the two sides of the manger near the heart of the V to hold the manger secure when in use. Disconnect the hook and the manger will unfold to be fairly flat, making it convenient for storage from year to year.

If you are planning a manger for children to play with, you will want it much smaller, and you will want to stabilize it more securely with wood pieces across the ends instead of a hook and eye fastener.[6]

—William Walker

manger by gluing together tongue depressors—or simply use an empty Christmas card box. "Children and adults alike could be rewarded for good deeds by being encouraged to place a small piece of 'straw' in the manger each day. (Toothpicks or shortened coffee stirrers could be used as straw.) Ideally, each family member would take note of the helpful behaviors of others and invite them to add a straw. The Christ child will certainly 'sleep in heavenly peace' when placed in the manger and welcomed into the world by so many good works and so much good will!"[4]

WHEN THE STORY NEEDS A FRESH LOOK

One year at a Christmas pageant rehearsal, a child exclaimed, "You mean we're doing the same story we did last year?"[5] I've even seen adult Sunday school teachers grimace at the prospect of teaching the Bible birth story yet *again*. One said to me, "What's left to be said?" I believe that the Christmas story always offers something new if we stop, really look at the miracle, and listen for the Lord's voice.

One way to help children gain a fresh look at the story of Jesus' birth is to read with them Barbara Robinson's *The Best Christmas Pageant Ever*. In this story no one wanted anything to do with the six Herdman children because they were so mean. Church was the one place the town children could get away from the Herdmans—until the Herdmans heard that refreshments were served at church. When they went for the refreshments, they learned about the annual Christmas pageant. They bribed and threatened the other children until they got the main parts.

The church members were aghast when they learned that the Herdman children would be playing the "holy" roles of Mary, Joseph, and the angel of the Lord. They thought, *Sweet, nice children should have those roles,* but they attended the pageant anyway. They wanted to see what those awful children would do.

What made that year's pageant "the best ever" was that the Herdmans interpreted Jesus' birth as a real event. They helped the church members see Jesus' birth for what it was: a live baby born to some weary strangers staying in a dirty, smelly stable.

Every aspect of the story is delightful, making it one the whole family will enjoy reading together. You might want to read aloud one of the seven chapters each night during the week before Christmas. Before starting the book say, "Imagine that you had never heard the Christmas story. You didn't know anything about it, and then somebody told you all about Mary and Joseph going to Bethlehem, the baby being born in a stable, the shepherds, the angels, the star, and the Wise Men. What would you think? What kind of questions would you have?"

The Best Christmas Pageant Ever is an inexpensive paperback published by Harper and Row as an Avon-Camelot book. It can be purchased at secular and Christian bookstores, and at school book fairs.

THERE'S MORE TO THE STORY

While younger children may need to learn the facts about Jesus' birth, older children—and sometimes adults—may need a review of the facts to keep the story of Jesus' birth separated from folklore. I have

BABY JESUS

Do you need a tiny baby Jesus to place in your small manger when it's filled with straw? Cut a Popsicle stick in half and draw a tiny face at the rounded end. Glue a flattened cotton ball or two to the back of the stick. For swaddling clothes, wrap some white gauze bandage around the head and body, leaving the face uncovered.

often reviewed the facts of Jesus' birth at Christmas parties by using the following quiz by Ron C. Carlson.[7]

All questions are based on the *King James Version* of the Bible. The answers are either true or false.

_____ 1. A heavenly messenger named Gabriel visited Mary.

_____ 2. The angel told Mary that the unborn baby's name would be "Jesus."

_____ 3. At first, Mary doubted the angel's message.

_____ 4. To protect her name and reputation, Mary told relatives and friends about the angel's message.

_____ 5. Mary visited her cousin Elizabeth three months prior to the birth of John the Baptist.

_____ 6. Joseph, a resident of Jerusalem, and Mary went to Bethlehem to pay tribute to Caesar.

_____ 7. Bethlehem is mentioned in the prophecy of Micah as the Messiah's birthplace.

_____ 8. Joseph was from the line of David, second king of Israel.

_____ 9. Three Wise Men came to see Jesus.

_____ 10. The Wise Men came from three different countries.

_____ 11. Religious leaders told the Wise Men where the Messiah would be born.

_____ 12. The Wise Men found Jesus in a stable.

_____ 13. The Wise Men presented three different gifts to Jesus.

_____ 14. A star guided shepherds to the manger.

RECOMMENDED READING

If your family enjoys reading *The Best Christmas Pageant Ever,* then you will also like *What Child Is This?* by Caroline B. Cooney. In this touching story, a foster child wants only one thing for Christmas—a family. In a season that celebrates miracles, is another miracle still possible? Can this little girl really find a family of her own?

_____15. An angel sang to the shepherds "Glory to God in the highest…"

_____16. The shepherds found Jesus lying in a manger.

_____17. The shepherds told others about Jesus.

_____18. Joseph, warned in a dream, fled to Nazareth.

_____19. The babies massacred in Bethlehem by King Herod were all two years old and under.

_____20. The Wise Men took the same route home as they did coming to Jerusalem and Bethlehem.

Answers to the Quiz

1. *True.* See Luke 1:26-27.

2. *True.* Matthew 1:21,25.

3. *True.* Luke 1:34 quotes Mary: "How shall this be, seeing I know not a man?"

4. *False.* Mary, throughout the Gospels, is said to "ponder these things in her heart." Nothing in Scripture indicates she tried to protect herself.

5. *True.* Luke 1:36-40.

6. *False.* Joseph resided in Nazareth, not Jerusalem (Luke 2:4).

7. *True.* See Micah 5:2, which is quoted by the religious leaders to King Herod in Matthew 2:4-6.

8. *True.* Matthew 1:6-16.

9. *False.* Scripture doesn't mention the number of Wise Men.

10. *False.* Scripture says only that the Wise Men were from the east.

11. *False.* Matthew 2:4-8. They told Herod, who told the Wise Men privately.

12. *False.* Matthew 2:11 says a house, not a stable.

13. *True.* Matthew 2:11 also lists three different types of gifts, "gold, frankincense, and myrrh."

14. *False.* It was the Wise Men who were led by the star (Matthew 2:2,7,10).

15. *False.* Luke 2:13-14 reads "...a multitude of the heavenly host praising God, and saying, Glory to God."

16. *True.* See Luke 2:16.

17. *True.* See Luke 2:17.

18. *False.* He left for Egypt and later returned to Nazareth (Matthew 2:14).

19. *True.* See Matthew 2:16.

20. *False.* See Matthew 2:12.

According to Carlson, a score of twenty correct answers is considered an exceptional performance. A score of nineteen is excellent, eighteen is good, and seventeen is fair. A score of sixteen or less indicates you need to read the story again.

I have used this quiz in my home with my own family, at gatherings of extended family, at Sunday school class socials, and in Sunday school classes. It is an effective way to get older teens and adults to think about the real story. Be careful, though. Occasionally I have had some people get upset when they find out that a star didn't lead the shepherds to Bethlehem or that the Bible doesn't say that there were *three* Wise Men!

Getting the facts straight can give us even more reason to celebrate the miracle of Christmas—the miracle of God becoming man, Emmanuel, God with us! Whatever kind of Advent calendar you choose and whether you make a life-size manger or a small one, you'll be helping your family prepare their hearts to welcome the newborn king!

CHAPTER 11

HONOR THY FATHER AND MOTHER

Mother's Day and Father's Day

Are you a mother of young children, looking for a way to help your children honor their father? Are you a husband wanting to help your children plan a special surprise for their mom? Perhaps you are a teenager, looking for personal, meaningful ways to honor your parents. You may be having your extended family for a Mother's Day or Father's Day gathering, and you want some meaningful way to recognize the family patriarch or matriarch.

Or maybe you feel that parenting isn't valued as it should be or you realize that parents can always use some encouragement, and you want to make sure that happens. If you teach a Sunday school class, you can use this chapter to help the members of your class express their appreciation both *for* their parents and *to* their parents. Perhaps you can gather the children of your neighborhood together and plan with them how to recognize their parents on Mother's Day and Father's Day. Or maybe you know of a weary and discouraged single parent who deserves honor and some practical help.

The art of appreciation, like the art of celebration, doesn't occur naturally. When we help children celebrate their mom or dad, we are helping them develop the art of appreciation, and in the process, we encourage the hearts of many parents. That's what Mother's Day

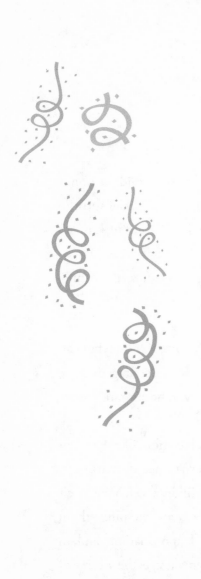

and Father's Day are about—making parents feel loved and honored so they will be refreshed in their roles and have treasured memories that will nourish them for years to come.

Make Personalized Greeting Cards

Stores will be packed with cards covered with flowers and gushing poetic feelings, but no card will be as treasured as the one a child makes. So use scraps of paper and clippings from magazines to craft cards for Mom and Dad.

- On the front of a folded piece of construction paper, write "I love you because…" or "You are a super mom (dad) because…" and then finish the statement on the inside of the card.

- Cut out a teddy bear shape and decorate it with markers, crayons, and stickers. Write on it "Good for free bear hugs."

- Make a very long paper necktie. Write on one side, "Here's the world's longest tie for the world's greatest dad! Happy Father's Day!"

- Cut off the front of a Wheaties cereal box. Over the athlete, paste a picture of Dad or Mom. Glue these words along the bottom: "My Hero, My Dad" or "My Mom, the Real Champion."

Honor your father and your mother, so that you may live long in the land the LORD your God is giving you.

Exodus 20:12, NIV

- Make an "I Promise" card. On the outside, print "Happy Father's Day." On the inside, print "I promise that I will…" and complete the sentence with something you will do such as "wash your car," "trim the hedges," "polish your shoes," or "say 'Yes sir,' and 'No sir' more often."

- Make a list of the words that describe your mother and use these to give her a "flower of words." Cut out a circle for the center of the flower and write across the middle, "Mother is…" Cut out petals, a stem, and leaves. On each petal, write

In *Virtue* magazine Barbara Baumgardner wrote about her mother appearing at her door with a thin packet of yellowed papers. "At 84, she was spending her first month in an apartment since selling the family home. Moving had meant sorting through the accumulated treasures of a lifetime. From one storage box came the packet she placed in my hand.

"Mom watched as I opened it to find two handwritten greetings I'd given her. I was eight when I wrote: 'Dear Mother, I love you for all the nice things you do for me. Thank you for all you have done. I will try to be a better girl after this. Love from Barbara.'

"The second was written a year later: 'Dear Mother, You have been such a help to me. You are the dearest mother I have and I hope to ever have. Today, since it is Mother's Day, I want to thank you for all you have done for me. It is so nice to have a mother like you. Your loving daughter, Barbara Jean Mize.'

"I glanced up at my mother, expecting her to chuckle with me. But she was serious as she simply stated, 'I really was loved, wasn't I?' "[2]

a word about your mother. Paste the flower, stem, and leaves on a big piece of colored paper. On the leaves, write "Happy Mother's Day!"[1]

Although most of these ideas for personalized greeting cards appear to be for children—and they do make good activities for children—we adults can make personalized greeting cards too. My husband has been honoring all of us through the years with cards he has made from clipping pictures and captions from magazines. They are so personal and clever that we much prefer them over store-bought cards.

SURROUND MOM OR DAD WITH SOUNDS OF LOVE

- *Make up a special blessing.* Before the meal that will honor Mom or Dad, usually Sunday breakfast or dinner, gather the children and compose a blessing together. Begin this way: "God, bless our mother (father). Reward her for her faithfulness to you and for her consistent love for her children. May each of her children recognize her worth and honor her example…" At the meal, read the blessing together. Save the blessing and use it year after year. If you want to use a special blessing at an extended family gathering, write one ahead of time and give a copy of it to everyone.

- *Record interviews that will bring smiles.* Record young children on audio or video answering questions about their parents.

Ask questions like "How tall is your dad?" "What is Mom's favorite color?" "What is her favorite food?" "What is Dad's favorite song?" "What does Mom do at work?" "Where does Daddy work?" "How old is your daddy?" and "What's your favorite thing to do with your mom?" Mom or Dad will enjoy hearing the delightful responses these kinds of questions prompt. The audio or videotape will be a treasured gift for years and years.

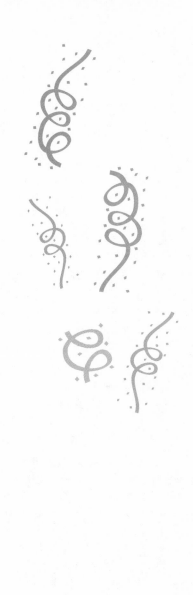

- *Show the difference one person makes.* If your celebration circle includes older children, teenagers, or young adults, ask each person at your celebration to respond to questions like these:

    What did your mother (or father) teach you about God?
    Did your father (or mother) ever rescue you? Describe the situation.
    What did your dad (or mom) teach you about hard work?
    What was the best piece of advice your father (or mother) ever gave you?
    What do you admire most about your father (or mother)?
    How are you similar to your mother (or father)?

- *Express appreciation and love in a song.* Using the melody for "Twinkle, Twinkle, Little Star" or some other familiar tune, write and sing a song for Mother or Father.

RECOMMENDED READING:

The four books listed below, although written for children, have a touching message that all ages love. Choose a child or an adult to read one of these books aloud before the family or group shares a special Mother's Day or Father's Day dessert. Everyone will be warmed and blessed by the story.

- *God Gave Us You* by Lisa Tawn Bergren. This delightful story assures children that they are truly a welcome, precious gift from God.

- *Love You Forever* by Robert Munsch. Although the story is about a mother and son, it is suitable for reading on either Mother's Day or Father's Day.

- *The Runaway Bunny* by Margaret Wise Brown. This story is especially appropriate for Mother's Day.

- *Guess How Much I Love You* by Sam McBratney. Read this one for Father's Day.

- *Ask people in the celebration circle to say why they love Mom or Dad.* Someone begins by saying, "I love Dad (or Mom) because he's (she's)…" Fill in the blank with whatever comes to mind. Maybe the first person says, "Because he goes to my ball games." The second person adds her own reason for loving Dad after she repeats the first person's reason: "I love Dad because he goes to our ball games and because…" The third person in the circle repeats the first two reasons and adds her own. This pattern continues around the circle, with participants repeating the reasons that have come before and adding their own. See if you can keep taking turns around the circle until it becomes impossible to remember all of the things said about Mom or Dad.[3] By the time this activity ends, your honoree will feel really loved and appreciated.

PRESENT MOM OR DAD WITH A SPECIAL AWARD

In 1907 Anna Jarvis started a campaign for a national Mother's Day because she loved her own mother so dearly and believed that adult children neglected their mothers. She wrote many letters and made many speeches in her efforts to get an official day designated for honoring mothers. "In explaining her idea, Anna said this should be a day 'to honor the best mother who ever lived—*your* mother.' "[4] When we think of *the best,* we think of special awards. Honor the father or mother at your house with a special award. Blow a trumpet, unfurl a scroll of parchment, read words of appreciation, and award special privileges for the day.

WISDOM FOR A NEW PARENT

Ask all the mothers and grandmothers in your extended family or church group to respond to this question: "What advice would you offer a new mother?" Likewise, ask the fathers and grandfathers, "What advice would you offer a new father?" If they write their answers on paper, put them in an album or folder. You could also record their answers on tape. Then present the album or tape to the new mother or father.

- *Mother or Father of the Year Award.* During your award ceremony, have family members list Mom or Dad's most appreciated and important accomplishments. Present the honored parent with a homemade trophy inscribed with "Mother (Father) of the Year" and the date.

- *King or Queen for a Day.* To start Mother's Day or Father's Day off right, present Mom or Dad with an official written declaration that he or she will be treated royally for a day. Read the declaration with authority and forcefulness. Of course, this calls for breakfast in bed, access to the remote, and no meal preparation or clean-up duties the rest of the day!

- *"World's Greatest Dad" or "Super Mom."* At an awards ceremony, have every family member state why they think Dad or Mom deserves this special award. Present a homemade trophy or a certificate with the honorary title and date on it.

GIVE GIFTS THAT GO ON GIVING

- *A "Feel Good" jar or box.* Record on strips of paper the ways your mother makes you feel good and put the strips in a decorated jar or box to give her on Mother's Day. The statements can begin with "You make me feel good when…," "I like it when…," or "My favorite thing that we do together is…" Mother can take a strip out whenever she wants to "feel good."

- *Kisses, kisses.* Give Mom or Dad a small basket of Xs cut out of heavy construction paper. With a ribbon, tie this note to the basket handle: "These Xs cut from paper are only good for this—hand one to me at anytime and you will get a kiss."[5] Os work, too, for hugs!

- *A magic broom.* Cut out a broom from a piece of heavy construction paper. Glue pine needles or straw on the bottom, and write a rhyme or promise on the handle, such as:

When my son Ben was in junior high, and at a time when I had been after him repeatedly to make his bed, he gave me a special award for Mother's Day. His computer-generated award read, "This certificate hereby gives you 30 days of unstoppable bed making unless, of course, there is a fire, tornado, or some other disaster."

"This is a Magic Broom. Put it on my pillow, and I will
clean my room."6

This is a Magic Broom. Stand it by my closet, and I will
sweep the garage.

This is a Magic Broom. Whenever you prop it by the
patio door, I will clean the patio.

- *Create a "Facts" jar* as a gift for Dad. On your own or with the rest of the family, decorate a jar or box and place slips of paper inside that state complimentary facts about Dad. Here are some examples:

  Dad is a good listener.

  Dad keeps our car running.

  Dad is terrific at washing the dishes.

  Dad is a great cook.

  Dad loves me.

  Dad is a good pitcher.

  Dad can read all these when the container is presented to him, or he can set his Facts Jar on his dresser, desk, or workbench, and take two or three out to read when he needs a boost.

CREATE A CLIMATE OF APPRECIATION

Mother's Day and Father's Day celebrations can spark gratitude for the daunting task of parenting in general—gratitude that can make every mother or father feel more appreciated. For the following activities,

A GIFT OF HUGS

I don't give Dad a tie on Father's Day 'cuz he says they make him sweat. I'll tell you what he'd rather have— a hug around his neck.7

FAMOUS MOTHERS IN THE BIBLE

We all recognize the names of these famous sons in the Bible, but do we know their mothers?

1. Who was the mother of Jesus?

2. Who was the mother of Cain and Abel?

3. Who was the mother of Isaac?

4. Who was the mother of Ishmael?

5. Who was the mother of Jacob?

6. Who was the mother of Esau?

7. In the Old Testament, who was Joseph's mother?

8. Who was the natural mother of Moses?

9. Who was Samuel's mother?

10. Who was Solomon's mother?

11. Who was the mother of John the Baptist?

12. Who was Timothy's mother?

Answers: 1. Mary, 2. Eve, 3. Sarah, 4. Hagar, 5. Rebekah, 6. Rebekah, 7. Rachel, 8. Jochebed, 9. Hannah, 10. Bathsheba, 11. Elizabeth, 12. Eunice

you may want to go beyond your own family to a wider circle of extended family and/or friends.

- *Create a cookbook.* Ask family members to submit a favorite recipe that your mother or father created or often makes. Ask them to also include reflections on that parent or any special memories of a time the recipe was prepared and served. Compile copies of all the entries in several binders and present them as gifts to the honoree and to all the family members who participated.

- *Recall famous sayings.* For fun when your extended family gathers, ask older children, teenagers, and adults to share words that they remember Mom and Dad saying over and over again. Include such family wisdom as "Spinach will make you grow big and strong," "I'm only doing this for your own good," and "If you can't say anything nice, don't say anything at all." Besides capturing the character of Mom or Dad, this activity will also contribute to your identity as a family.

- *Recognize your heritage by playing the "begotten" game.* The Bible describes family lineage in terms of who begot whom, and we can do something similar. When your extended family gathers, ask each member to first say his or her own name, then Dad's name, and finally something interesting about

Dad. The lineage could start, for example with Anne saying, "Anne, begotten by William, who has a great sense of humor." Each person around the celebration circle does the same for his or her father. That's Round #1. In Round #2, participants say their name and Dad's name, but then they add Grandpa's name and something interesting about him. Anne might say, "Anne, begotten by William, begotten of Stanley, who fought in France during the Second World War." If your family is rich in stories about their ancestors, try a third round, going back another generation to the great-grandfather.[8] Since some societies do trace their lineage through the mothers, you can also use this game on Mother's Day and acknowledge your heritage through Mom, Grandma, and Great-grandma.

- *Take notice of biblical mothers and fathers.* For some reflective fun at the dinner table or in the family room after dessert, take one of the short quizzes on these two pages.

FAMOUS FATHERS IN THE BIBLE

Match the father with the correct offspring.

____	1. Adam	A. Joseph
____	2. Noah	B. John the Baptist
____	3. Abraham	C. Jacob
____	4. Isaac	D. James and John
____	5. Jacob	E. Solomon
____	6. Zechariah	F. Isaac and Ishmael
____	7. Zebedee	G. Ham, Shem, and Japheth
____	8. David	H. Cain, Abel, and Seth

Answers: 1. H, 2. G, 3. F, 4. C, 5. A, 6. B, 7. D, 8. E

One more suggestion for adding meaning to your Mother's Day and Father's Day celebration. Spend time in prayer! Thank your heavenly Father for the parents he gave you—and then pray for Mom and Dad.

CHAPTER 12

BEYOND THE CAKE AND ICE CREAM

Birthdays

When my friend Kay's brother turned five years old, his mother was sick and couldn't bake him a birthday cake. He went to her bedside and cried, "I didn't see my birthday!" Decorations, cakes, and gifts help us "see" our birthdays. To celebrate with meaning enables the honoree to "see" how he is appreciated, loved, and valued.

YOU DID THIS FOR ME?

To make a birthday celebration special, think about the person you want to honor. What would he or she like to do to celebrate this year? Some years you may want the birthday celebration to be a surprise, but at other times you may want to ask for specifics from the birthday boy or girl. Does he want to invite all his school friends to a party? Would she like a slumber party with three good friends—or a simple sleepover with her best friend? Is he comfortable in large groups—or would he prefer cele-brating with family members? Before you plan your birthday celebration, make sure you're arranging something the person you are honoring would truly enjoy.

As you begin to plan, consider these additional ideas for making birthdays special:

- *King or Queen for a Day.* Declare the birthday person King or Queen for the Day. Greet him or her first thing in the morning with a special crown. You or your

kids can make the crown out of cardboard, cover it with pasta, and spray paint it gold. Escort the honoree to a special breakfast where he or she sits in the chair of honor.

- *Fly a birthday flag.* Design and create a birthday flag that represents the honoree's interests and special abilities. Use his or her favorite colors and fly the flag from sunup to sundown on the big day. You might even have a flag-raising and flag-lowering where you sing a favorite song or make up a cheer.[2]

- *"Only me" birthday dinner out.* Sometimes a celebration is more meaningful when others are not around. Dinner alone with just the birthday person—parents and child, friend with friend—can be a nice change. A child with several siblings, for instance, will value the time when he can talk without others interrupting and have his parents' undivided attention. What a thoughtful gift!

ENCOURAGING WORDS, LOVING SUPPORT

- *How do I affirm thee? Let me count the ways.* Number a stack of three-by-five-inch index cards—one for each year being celebrated—then place them on the table. Ask everyone at the celebration to share affirmations or compliments for the birthday person. With each affirmation, the speaker turns over a card. Participants might say things like, "You really persevered with the swim team even when the competition was really tough." "You bring so much laughter to our lives. Your jokes and sense of humor make us smile." Or "I admire the way you respond to challenges. I learn by watching you."

- *Let me write the ways.* Enclose a three-by-five-inch index card with the party invitations. Ask recipients to write an affirmation or a prayer of thanksgiving for the birthday honoree and

What makes a birthday happy lies in the creativity brought into play. It doesn't take a lot of money, and it often doesn't take much time or energy (although it can, of course, include a great deal of all three). The key lies in one's ability to get out of one's self and think of the one being honored, the ability to remember him or her in a special or imaginative way.... That aspect of a birthday means the world to the recipient and, in reflecting upon it or in telling about it to others...all the colorful and enriching details will be remembered because "somebody cared that much about me."[1]

—Luci Swindoll, *You Bring the Confetti, God Brings the Joy*

to bring the card with them to the celebration. Designate a time at the party for guests to read what they wrote. Have them place the affirmations and prayers in a basket or tie them together with ribbon as a special gift for the birthday person.

- *Birthday letters.* Write the birthday person a letter, summing up the last year of his or her life. Write about important events, what admirable character traits you noted about the person (his or her courage, perseverance, etc.), what you expect for his or her future, and how you feel about that person. If you are honoring a young child, write a letter every year and place it in a special binder that you can give the child when he or she leaves home. You might want to tuck in a picture of the child each year as well.

- *Candles and blessings.* At the end of the meal, place the birthday cake on a table in the center of the room. Distribute birthday candles to all the guests. Place a large, round white candle beside the cake and light the candle. Ask guests, one by one, to light his or her smaller candle in the flame of the large candle, place it on the top of the birthday cake, and then offer a blessing for the birthday person. Each blessing could begin with the words "May the Lord bless you with…" When every person has placed a candle on the cake and given a blessing, ask everyone to join hands and form a large circle around the cake to sing "Happy Birthday."[3]

- *Birthday Center Awards.* Honor the birthday person's performance, efforts, or achievements with a ceremony similar to the Kennedy Center Awards. Each year the Kennedy Center honors singers, filmmakers, composers, actors, producers, and directors with an overview of their life's work, remembrances from friends and family members, and a performance of some of their works by other talented people. You can do something similar at home. First, hang a homemade medallion around the birthday person's neck and ask him or her to sit in a place of honor. Give a brief summary of the honoree's life, noting special milestones or accomplishments ("Julie accepted Jesus into her heart when she was six" or "Billy got his first job—mowing yards—when he was fourteen. He mowed ten yards each week, and his customers paid him high compliments!") Display that person's artwork, read letters from camp or selected "writings" from school compositions, play favorite songs, or tell some of his or her favorite jokes.

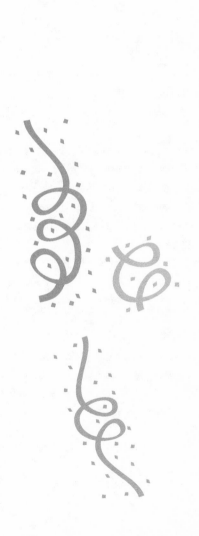

- *Oldest child ceremony.* The firstborn child has special advantages, including his parents' undivided attention and the doting adoration of his grandparents. But the oldest child also paves the way for his siblings. Younger brothers and/or sisters observe the oldest child and learn from him or her. To honor the oldest child, have younger siblings explain, "What I Learned from My Older Brother (Sister)."

Birthdays always have been very special at our house. Every birthday person gets breakfast in bed, and is king or queen for that day. We decorate the house with balloons and streamers, and brightly decorate the pile of gifts. We either use the best china and silver or a carefully selected theme of birthday plates, napkins, and tablecloth. Then we let the birthday person choose his or her very favorite menu and birthday dessert, and gather together as many members of the family who possibly can be there to celebrate....

We always include the birthday prayer. This is giving thanks to God for giving us that special person, and then evoking God's special blessing on him or her for the coming year. This usually is prayed by an 'elder' of the family—dad, mom, grandfather, grandmother, or great-grandmother.[4]

—Evelyn Christenson,
What Happens When We Pray for Our Families

• *Pray a special birthday prayer.* Prepare a prayer to pray at the birthday celebration or ask someone to prepare one. Include thanksgiving both for the honoree and for the events of the past year. Be specific. Also ask God to guide and bless him or her in the year ahead. You can read specially selected Bible verses before the prayer or include them as part of the prayer.

As another option, you could open (or close) your celebration by inviting attendees to pray for the birthday person. Begin by reading Psalm 139:13-16 and saying, "These words speak of God's great love for you whom he so wonderfully fashioned. And we are so glad that he has put you in our lives." After the closing amen, remind the person that he or she is a great gift to everyone gathered and that this birthday is truly an occasion for celebration!

Past and Future Attention in the Present

• *Past connection.* In *The Education of Little Tree*, Forrest Carter writes about the Cherokee custom of telling a child, during his or her birthday season, about his birthplace, his father's doings, and his mother's love. On your child's birthday, share the story of his birth or adoption. Include details like where you were living at the time, what work you were involved in, and what life was like for your family then. Put into words the love—both from God and your family—that brought him or her into your home.

- *Long line of love.* Ask guests to line up according to how long they have known the honored guest (mothers, fathers, sisters, brothers, followed by childhood friends, classmates, etc.). Ask each person to tell how long he or she has known the birthday person, how they met, and their current connection.

- *A photo quiz.* Put together a large collection of photos centering around the honoree. Mount these on poster board, give each picture a number, and hang the poster in a prominent place. When the guests arrive, give each one a pencil and a

THE NIGHT YOU WERE BORN

Each year on his birthday for over forty years, Philip Gulley's father told him the "story" of his birth. It was a dramatic (and somewhat exaggerated) account involving a terrible snowstorm, frostbite, swirling red lights, a siren's wail, and a police escort to the hospital. The father always ended the story the same way: "You had a police escort to the hospital. Not everyone can say that. That makes you special."

About that story, Gulley writes, "In my teenage years, when my father and I were at odds, I would remember how he suffered frostbite to bring me safely into this world...and my heart would soften. I was a skinny child, the target of bullies. When beaten up and ridiculed, I would take comfort in the fact that I was ushered into this world with a police escort and they were not. It was a wonderful gift my father gave me, that story. He could not give me wealth or fame to ease my way, so he gave me that story and it provided a deep consolation."[5]

sheet of paper on which you have printed the numbers and a short question for each number: "Where was Tom when this picture was taken?" "How old was Tom here?" "What was the occasion of this photo?"

- *How well do you know the birthday boy or girl?* Make up a quiz about the honoree, asking questions such as "Where was Linda born?" "What are her favorite foods?" "What is her favorite song?" etc. The honored guest will bask in the attention and delight in sharing with her friends some of the details of her life.

- *Future look.* Some birthdays will represent a significant change for the person being honored. (The thirteenth, sixteenth, eighteenth, twenty-first, and thirtieth birthdays are generally considered momentous.) If your guests are older than the honoree, have them offer words of wisdom for the next stage of life. Ben turned eighteen in the spring. He would soon graduate from high school and head off to college. At his birthday dinner, I asked his older brothers to give him some advice about being a college student. Their words of wisdom included, "Study hard, don't eat too much pizza, get a calling card, confront your roommates right away about problems, and don't overextend yourself."

You could also ask guests to guess what the future holds for the birthday person: "Let's go around the table and say what we think John will be doing five years from now."

As a variation on this theme, include a three-by-five-inch index card with your invitation. On the front of the card, print this verse:

Here are just some little thoughts
Concerning your life's next span.
May you and God together
Concoct a wonderful plan.

Leave the other side blank, and ask guests to use that space to record their predictions, then bring the completed cards to your celebration dinner or party. Invite guests to read their predictions aloud, then present the cards to the honoree. Years later he or she can look back on these to see how accurate they were.

Not only is a birthday an exciting and anticipated day, but your enthusiasm and planning can make it a memorable one as well. Long after the candles are blown out, the glow of love expressed through special treatment, encouraging words, and thoughtful prayers will warm the heart of the recipient, making him or her feel appreciated, loved, and valued. What better birthday gift could be given?

Here's a quiz I compiled for my son Ben's birthday party when he was a junior in high school.

1. What is Ben's middle name?

2. In what city was he born?

3. Name three places Ben has lived.

4. What is the high school swim team's nickname for Ben?

5. What awards has he received as a swimmer?

6. What is Ben's favorite food?

7. What's his favorite kind of music?

8. What's his favorite hymn?

9. What's his favorite sport to watch on television?

10. What's Ben's favorite sport to play?

11. What accident left Ben scarred for life?

12. What's the title of Ben's favorite video?

CHAPTER 13

AFTER THE TASSEL IS MOVED

Graduations

When my sons graduated from high school, their large classes were seated on the football field, and family members and friends sat in the bleachers. During one of the graduation ceremonies, some families left as soon as their child received a diploma. Our family was sitting in the third row, and the steady stream of people parading before us blocked our view. I wanted to yell, "Sit down so I can see *my* son graduate." Such feelings hardly make for a meaningful occasion, yet I wanted it to be meaningful.

Graduation marks an important milestone in a person's life. It's a major accomplishment that deserves to be recognized and celebrated.

Make your family member or friend's graduation a meaningful occasion by planning a time for people of faith to surround him or her with support, joy, and affirmation.

WHAT DOES THE GRADUATE WANT?

When our sons graduated from high school, they wanted to invite their friends to celebrate with them, and my husband and I wanted to invite our friends, so after each graduation, we held an open house. When my sons graduated from college, I asked each of them if they wanted an

Oh, the joy of accomplishment!...We like to finish things, don't we? And to absolutely know we've finished, there's nothing like beating the drums, popping the corks, throwing the confetti, and commemorating the victory.[1]
—Luci Swindoll, *You Bring the Confetti, God Brings the Joy*

open house again. All three opted for small dinner parties with just two or three close friends and our family of five.

To truly honor a person—whatever the occasion—we need to consider what pleases him or her. When we consult and plan with the graduate, we make the graduate feel recognized as a unique and special individual.

CREATE A WINNER'S CIRCLE

If your graduate chooses a small celebration, create a winner's circle. Gather your family members and guests around a table to share brunch, lunch, or dinner. Sometime during the meal invite your graduate to talk about his or her plans, dreams, and perhaps even fears about the future. Guide the conversation by asking your graduate questions such as these:

- What was the hardest part of your high school (or college) career?

- Did you ever think about quitting?

- What was the most important lesson you learned in high school (or college)?

- What are your plans for the future?

When Ben graduated from Marine Basic Training and his brother Joel received his master's degree, we had a joint celebration. We asked them:

- What was the lowest moment you experienced?

- What was the highest moment?

- What was your biggest fear when you started?

- Now that you've finished, what are you proudest of?

- How did your experience meet or not meet your expectations?

We honor our graduates when we ask them questions like these and listen attentively to their responses. This kind of conversation not only helps them review their experiences, but it also lets them know we're celebrating their accomplishments.

MEANINGFUL GIFTS

- *Give gifts that last.* Choose for graduates a gift that will last (a Bible, a book by their—or your—favorite writer) or a gift that will help them fulfill their future plans. If you give a book, write a personal inscription in the front, sign it, and date it. The gift can be a symbol of your love and blessing to the graduate.

- *Give gifts of time.* When Ben's open house was over and the last guests had gone, I had some time alone with him. I gave him a book of fiction—a good read I thought he would enjoy. In it I wrote a note about how much I had treasured reading books aloud with him in the past and how I looked forward to sharing one more good story with him before he left for college. Part of my gift was the promise to reserve time for reading the book with him during the summer.

- *Give a gift of memories.* Collect memorabilia and photos of your graduate and assemble them attractively in a scrapbook. When Joel graduated from college as a music performance

When we create special celebrations to affirm those we love, we speak for God who says you are loved and cared for.[2]
—Jeanne Hunt, *Holy Bells and Wonderful Smells*

major, Cathy, one of his close friends, gave him a scrapbook containing all the programs and posters from the recitals and concerts he had participated in during his five years there. When she handed Joel the gift, it was as if she was saying, "Here is what you have accomplished. Congratulations! You have done well!"

- *Give a personalized diploma.* Design a diploma that will uniquely represent the graduate's high school or college experience. My husband designed a debt-free diploma for our oldest son, Jim, when he graduated from college. We were so glad he could graduate without having student loans to repay. It was certainly cause for celebration!

  In contrast to the usual black lettering on white paper, you might make your diploma more personal by incorporating color and using interesting border icons and illustrations. If your daughter is a musician, you could have a border of musical notes or sketches of the instruments she plays. Computer graphics software offers many possibilities for personalizing diplomas.

Bless Your Graduate

- Ask friends, relatives, and teachers to write personal keepsake letters commending your graduate. Assemble the letters in a notebook or specially decorated box and give it to your child on graduation day.

- If your graduate plans to attend college, buy some blue exam books. Place two or three blue books and several pens around the party area. Ask guests to write memories about your graduate. People might write, "I remember when nine-year-old John made a profession of faith." or "In seventh grade, Sarah said she would become the first woman president of the United States."

- Ask guests to offer bits of advice. If the gathering is small, these thoughts can be shared verbally. If the gathering is large, have index cards or note cards and pens available for guests to write on sometime during the party. Collect these in a basket or decorated box and give it to the graduate.

- In biblical times fathers traditionally sent their children off with a blessing, sometimes outlining their inheritance but also recognizing their independence. Pronounce a blessing on your graduate at the end of a commemorative meal, after the open house, or before leaving for the graduation ceremonies.

- When believers in the early church were embarking on a special task, other believers laid hands on them and prayed over them. Your graduate is embarking on a new stage of life. So gather around your child, offer thanks for what he or she has already accomplished, and then ask God to guide and bless him or her in the future.

HIGH SCHOOL GRADUATION: A RITE OF PASSAGE

Nearly every society has some ritual to mark the passage from childhood to adulthood. In our society, high school graduation ceremonies serve that purpose. So give your child a symbol that represents what this transition from childhood to adulthood means. Here are some ideas:

- One mother gave her son a box that held her apron strings, communicating her recognition of his emancipation.

- If *you* are ready, hand over the key to the front door of your home to signify that you are giving your graduate the right to come and go as he or she pleases.

TRADITIONAL BLESSING

May the Lord bless and protect you;
may the Lord's face radiate
*   with joy because of you;*
may he be gracious to you,
show you his favor,
*   and give you his peace.*

Numbers 6:24–26 (TLB)

• One family gave their daughter a ring with three small stones. They told her, "As you go far from home, wear this ring and remember that you are like the middle stone of this setting, surrounded on both sides by our love."[3]

CELEBRATING YESTERDAYS AND ANTICIPATING TOMORROWS

At graduation time we look back as well as forward. In one breath, people say to the graduate, "Congratulations! Good job! Way to go!" In the next breath, they ask, "What are you going to do now? Are you going to college? Are you going into the military? Where are you going to work? What do you want to do?"

Your graduate will welcome the opportunity to look back on his or her life, and so will your guests—those family members and friends who may not have been there for all the important events.

• Write a short biography of your graduate's life to read aloud at the graduation party.

• Prepare a brief slide show or compile video clips of the graduate at different moments of his or her life.

• Display memorabilia and photos (even scrapbooks and photo albums) so guests can get a sense of your graduate's life.

As you celebrate the past, celebrate the future as well. Graduation means closure because the graduate has reached a goal. But, appropriately, graduation is also called "commencement" because graduates are beginning their new lives.

- Have your guests talk about what they see the graduate doing in the future. Everyone (and perhaps the honoree most of all) will enjoy hearing their predictions. Take notes as the people share so that your son or daughter will have a written record. If the group is large, ask guests to write down their thoughts for the graduate to look at later. Ten years down the road, your graduate will enjoy reading the predictions and seeing which came true.

- Read aloud *Oh, the Places You'll Go* by Dr. Seuss. People of all ages enjoy this book. It captures the sense of adventure that awaits your graduate.

- Seemingly endless options for the future can intimidate anyone, but it can be particularly frightening for a high school graduate. Assure your child of God's loving presence and guidance by having guests write encouraging Bible verses on index cards. Give them to your graduate or read them aloud.

BIBLE VERSES THAT WILL ENCOURAGE GRADUATES

Deuteronomy 31:8

Psalm 37:4

Proverbs 3:5-6

Isaiah 30:21

Jeremiah 29:11

Matthew 6:33

Matthew 7:7

Romans 8:28

Romans 8:38-39

Hebrews 13:5

To learn means to accept the postulate that life did not begin at my birth. Others have been here before me, and I walk in their footsteps. The books I have read were composed by generations of fathers and sons, mothers and daughters, teachers and disciples. I am the sum total of their experiences, their quests. And so are you.[4]

—Elie Wiesel, *Parade Magazine*

As with any of life's crossroads, a high school or college graduation is a wonderful occasion for looking back and thanking God for his great faithfulness. It's also a time to look forward in anticipation of the blessings God has in store and the guidance he will grant. You can add these elements to a graduation party with scripture and prayer, always appropriate as gifts of love and encouragement.

CHAPTER 14

HAPPY ANNIVERSARY TO US...AND TO OTHERS

Wedding Anniversaries

A wedding anniversary is definitely a time to stop and take notice! These days, staying married is a major accomplishment. Let's celebrate that achievement by focusing on what's right in our marriages, expressing gratitude to God and our spouse for the life we've built together, affirming our loyalty to each other, acknowledging God's faithfulness to us, kindling our love, and renewing our commitment. Let's express our joy and gratitude at still being married—and let's dream together about the future. If we're honoring our parents or friends on their anniversaries, we can celebrate with them as well. In this chapter you'll find ideas for marking other people's anniversaries as well as for the most important anniversaries of all—your own!

JUST THE TWO OF US

Little Things Mean a Lot

Year in and year out, most couples opt for private anniversary celebrations: dinner out at an expensive restaurant, a return to "their special place," a cruise, an overnight at a bed-and-breakfast, or a canoe trip down a lazy river. For many couples, a special event like this is celebration enough, but others want to acknowledge their fidelity and renew their commitment to each other.

- *An add-on gift.* Give your spouse something that you can "add on to" with each wedding anniversary, something very special that symbolizes your commitment to each other. You might give a cultured pearl or other semi-precious stone that can one day be made into a bracelet or necklace, a leather-bound classic to begin a personal library, or a silk rose that will become a beautiful bouquet as the years pass.[2]

- *Unity candle.* Bring out the unity candle from your wedding, light it, and put it on the dinner table as you celebrate a special anniversary dinner at home. When you light the candle, talk together about how this symbol has been realized in your marriage. (If this becomes a yearly ritual, you might limit your focus to the past year.)

- *Wedding mementos.* Most of us save items from our weddings: photographs, videos, cards, the guest book, etc. Reviewing these items can rekindle many of the feelings of that special day. Nanci and Doyle sometimes take along the guest book and cards from their wedding to read when they go out to celebrate their anniversary. The thoughts of love and the people's prayers encourage them and remind them of what they wanted their marriage to be, thus renewing their determination to continue.

Mark and Katie, who used a special antique goblet for taking Communion in their wedding ceremony, bring out the goblet every anniversary, whatever they're doing that year to celebrate. Whether

Throughout Scripture, there is a distinct current of celebration, especially as God reveals His intention in creating marriage. When God fashioned Eve and brought her to Adam, they celebrated (Genesis 2:22-25). When Ruth and Boaz were united, there was jubilation (Ruth 4:14). Solomon and Shulamith rejoiced their way through Song of Songs, from the first word in chapter one to the last word in chapter eight. Proverbs is full of exhortations to married couples to enjoy their relationship. Proverbs 5:18 is certainly direct: "May your fountain be blessed, and may you rejoice in the wife of your youth." "Rejoice" means to reel as though intoxicated. No doubt about it! God's talking about celebration![1]

—Harold and Bette Gillogly, *HomeLife*

they're on the beach, in a hotel, or at home, out comes the goblet! It helps them both celebrate how far they have come and rededicate themselves to each other and to Christ.

Not Just Any Night Out

A relaxed candlelight dinner helps rekindle the fragile flame of love often buffeted by job and family pressures. Forgo the usual talk about schedules, carpooling, and bills, and focus instead on the intimate and less practical aspects of your marriage. For some, this kind of conversation comes naturally; for others, it takes a bit of effort. Here are some ideas for making your evening out meaningful:

- *Make dinner reservations at a special place.* If possible, choose a restaurant that reminds you of a place you ate at during your honeymoon.

- *Pretend the two of you are on a first date.* Have the husband pick up the wife at the house, as if he were calling on her for the first time. Pretend that you have just met and tell each other about yourselves as if you don't know each other.

- *Reframe earlier experiences by looking for the humor.* If you have been married for some time, you have undoubtedly shared some less-than-pleasant experiences. Look back at some of those. Add a little forgiveness, take yourselves less seriously,

Rituals tend to direct energy toward a larger goal. They bring a balance of material and spiritual energies. Personalized ceremonies also create a sense of continuity and tradition. Couples whose marriages flourish over the years will probably have consciously or unconsciously created special rituals that they regularly carry out. Love can age and grow richer and more mellow, just like a fine wine. Even with long-time friends, the love softens with comfort and deepens with tenderness. Acknowledging and honoring these feelings can enhance the relationship.[3]

—Sydney Barbara Metrick, *I Do*

A successful marriage requires falling in love many times, always with the same person.[4]
—Migon McLaughlin, as quoted in
The Creative Wedding Idea Book

"Remember When" can be solemn or silly, leave us laughing or with a lump in our throat, but it always unites us, link by link, to the past we share.[5]
—Judith Viorst, *Redbook*

and find the humor in the situation. This exercise will help ease tension and marriage fatigue as well as renew your faith in each other and your marriage.

• *Share love letters.* Prior to the evening out, both of you can write down what good things you see in your marriage and/or what you appreciate about your spouse. Over coffee and dessert, or as the evening of celebration ends, read your letters to each other.

• *Pray together.* Offer thanks for your good memories. Let God know how grateful you are for the events that he has woven into the fabric of your marriage. Thank him for the uniqueness of your spouse.

• *Play "Remember When."* Remember when you first met, what you did on your first date, when you fell in love, when he proposed, when you rented your first apartment, when you brought the babies home from the hospital, and so on.

Finances Tight?

What if you would like a meal out, but can't afford it? Have an elegant meal at home instead. Plan the menu together, cook together, and enjoy the meal together in a beautiful setting: Include a lace or linen tablecloth, your best dishes, and candlelight. If possible, wear your wedding dress for this special meal. You'll add a sense of celebra-

tion to the evening, and it's a great chance to wear what was probably a very expensive dress!

If you have children at home, consider including them in the celebration. Depending on their ages, children can help prepare the meal, set the table, make cards for you, and listen as you "remember when." Your stories will kindle your love for each other as well as give your children knowledge of family history and a sense of security.

It's Party Time!

Some couples want to celebrate their marriages in a big way, especially at milestone anniversaries such as the fifth, tenth, twentieth, twenty-fifth, thirtieth, fortieth, and fiftieth. At these times we may want to

Building a history together, chapter by chapter, every couple creates a "story," and couples in long marriages respect their own stories—about how they met, their private jokes, their code words and rituals, even the sadnesses they shared. Theirs is not mere nostalgia, but an attachment to the significance of their past and of the time spent together.[6]
—Francine Klagsbrun, *Reader's Digest*

invite others to join us in honoring our marriage. Here are several ways to add meaning to those celebrations:

- *Plant a tree.* Choose an oak for solidarity, a pine for your "evergreen" relationship, or a flaming red maple for your burning passion. "One of you should make a speech: 'We have been married for five years now. And in that time, our love for each other has grown, more than we could ever have imagined. We're planting this tree tonight as a symbol of our love—living, growing, weathering all kinds of storms, and withstanding the tests of time.'... When the planting is completed, someone may propose a toast: 'To Dave and Amy—may their marriage continue to grow and prosper—like this tree!' "[7]

- *Share your history.* People in long marriages value their history together, and sometimes they want to share parts of that history with family and friends. They want to tell others about their courtship, significant events in their lives, lessons they've learned, and God's faithfulness to them through the years. A dinner party, where everyone can sit facing each other, makes a good setting for this kind of sharing.

  When Ted and Linda celebrated their twenty-fifth wedding anniversary, they invited guests to dress as someone famous from the past twenty-five years. On one wall they posted a horizontal scroll that displayed a time line of events in their marriage. Guests were invited to sign in at the point where they met the couple. They also had a treasure hunt of art objects they had collected during their marriage. They had scattered them throughout the house and gave guests clues for where to find the "treasures."

- *Renew your wedding vows.* Renewing your vows every few years rekindles your commitment to God, each other, and your marriage. It can also remind you of what you wanted your marriage to be like. This ritual takes on more significance when you invite people to witness the ceremony. Assemble your guests around you as you repeat your original wedding vows to each other.

  For their twenty-fifth wedding anniversary celebration, Bob and Charlotte went beyond merely repeating their vows. They reenacted their original wedding ceremony, with Charlotte surprising Bob by wearing her wedding gown. This time their children took part in the service by presenting the special music and readings.

ANNIVERSARY CELEBRATIONS FOR OTHERS

Sometimes we want to honor others who are celebrating an anniversary. The twenty-fifth and fiftieth wedding anniversaries are popular occasions for grand celebrations for parents or friends.

- Make a collage of photographs, items reflecting their work and hobbies, maps of places the couple has traveled, and other souvenirs from their lives. The collage should reflect the growth of the two as individuals, the two as a couple, and the two of them as mother and father, aunt and uncle, even grandmother and grandfather through the years.

• Make a basket of memories and give it to the couple. Include menus from the restaurant where he proposed or the spots where they've celebrated in the past, special little mementos that bring back memories of wonderful times, photographs, and a cassette of "their song" or a CD of love songs. Arrange the mementos in a wicker basket lined with doilies or wrapping paper.

• Secretly write to the couple's friends and ask them to write down what the couple means to them and/or record memories of times they've shared. Enclose a self-addressed stamped envelope as well as the paper to write on so that all the sheets will match when you put them in a scrapbook.

• As part of an open house or dinner party, have a program in honor of the married couple. (Some ideas are listed below.) On the invitation be sure to tell what time the program will be held. (I failed to do this when my parents celebrated their fiftieth wedding anniversary. The entrance was right beside the program area. As family members were speaking and singing

before the group, visitors streamed in, distracting both the
audience and the honorees.)

Program Ideas

• Introduce all the family members in attendance. Many in the
audience of a couple celebrating their fiftieth wedding
anniversary may not know the couple's children and grandchildren.

AN ANNIVERSARY PROGRAM PRAYER

Father, we thank you for this occasion today when we gather to celebrate the marriage of _____ and _____. We're glad you brought these two together! Thank you for walking with them through the good times and the hard times. They've dried each other's tears and applauded each other's successes. Today we ask that you bless our efforts to celebrate them because it has been our pleasure to know this couple, to see their love for you and for each other, to learn from their example, and to be inspired by their commitment to each other during their _____ years of marriage. On this day, help them to know how special they are to us and how noteworthy their achievement is. As they begin another year together, help them to continue to grow in their love and appreciation for each other. We pray you will give them many more happy years together.

- Introduce any members of the original wedding party who are present.

- Ask for oral tributes to the couple. (You might ask people in advance so that a few folks are ready to share at this time.)

- Display scrapbooks and selected photos of the couple's life together.

- Have a "This is Your Life" presentation. Involve people who were in the wedding or who were a part of significant events early in the marriage or relationship. Voices of the individuals can be heard from offstage, and the couple can guess who is speaking.

- If the group is not too large, play "I've Got a Memory." Before the program, print out words that will stir memories of stories about the couple: *sailboat, the tornado of 1990, snake in the car, new puppy, twelve inches of snow, duck eggs,* and so on. Each guest will draw a slip and briefly recall the situation, ideally with as much humor as possible.[8]

- In a large bag, basket, or box, collect symbols of the couple's years together: a cradle, trophies, a dog collar, a fishing pole, a cap, a souvenir from Niagara Falls, etc. Take each item out one by one and hold it up for the guests to view. Offer whimsical or nostalgic comments on these symbols of a very special marriage.[9]

• Play music that is significant to the couple.

• Make up songs about the couple and sing them as part of the program. In honor of Dean and Barbara Spencer's December anniversary, their children and grandchildren wrote and sang songs about them to the tune of familiar Christmas carols. Here's one example to the tune of "Hark! The Herald Angels Sing":

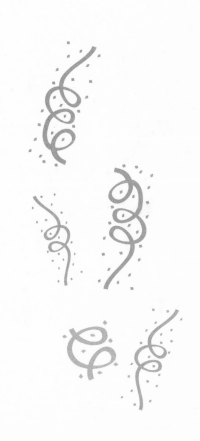

> *It was nineteen fifty-five*
> *None of us was yet alive*
> *That our grandma and our grandpa*
> *Went to church to tie the knot.*
>
> *One by one we all appeared*
> *Throughout the next forty years*
> *Now you're stuck and we won't leave*
> *You started it on Christmas Eve.*
>
> *So you have yourself to blame,*
> *We're glad you did it just the same.*[10]

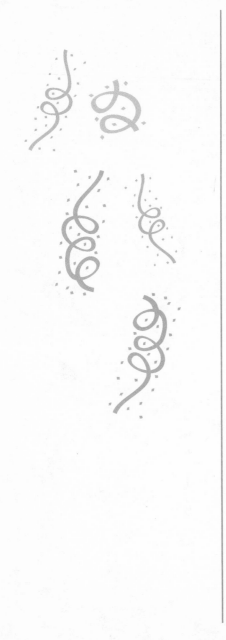

- Give an anniversary gift that has significance and meaning. For example, the grandchildren could give their grandparents a clock as thanks for all the time they spend with them.

- Interview the couple. Keep this short, to twenty minutes or less. If the couple is shy, videotape the interview ahead of time. Ask questions like:

  How did you meet?

  What attracted you to each other?

  What did you do on dates?

  Was there a particular song that was "your song"? What was it?

  Describe your wedding. Who was in it? What were the colors? Who performed the ceremony? Were there any glitches or embarrassing/ humorous moments?

  What were the best years of your marriage? Why?

  What were the hardest years? What made them hard— and what kept you going?

  What's the fondest memory you have of your marriage?

  What advice would you give to couples who are getting married today?

- Several weeks before the celebration start videotaping the recollections of a few friends and family members who have been close to the couple since before they were married. Ask them about the couple's courtship days. "Ask questions such as, How did they meet? Did they have lovers' spats? Was their romance hot and passionate or sweet and romantic? Who proposed? and What was the wedding day like? Edit the tape for viewing at the party."[11]

Designed by God, marriage is indeed worth celebrating! My hope is that these ideas will help rekindle and strengthen the love between husbands and wives. May these ideas also offer opportunities to encourage couples as they look back on where the Lord has taken them and anticipate the blessings he has for them in the future.

WHEN WE PLAN, WE GAIN

We had such fun preparing for [our parents' fiftieth wedding anniversary], enjoying the occasion to be together, but it was much more. I had the distinct feeling of being a long-distance runner in a relay: We, the three married children, were now taking up the long tradition and carrying it on. Knowing how fragile marriage is, I wondered where we would be years from now. But I only wondered for a moment, for there they were—a testimonial to enduring solidarity and love. I accepted being a runner, being part of the relay, carrying on the tradition.[12]

—Neno O'Neill, *Reader's Digest*

CHAPTER 15

CAPTURE THE MOMENT

Your Unique Celebrations

hristmas, Easter, Fourth of July, Mother's Day, Father's Day, birthdays, graduations, and anniversaries are occasions most people celebrate. But once you discover the joy that comes when you celebrate with meaning, you may want to celebrate events that the rest of the world doesn't recognize—moments that are special just to your family or friends. You may want to celebrate events such as these:

- *Moving to a new home.* One military wife always packed a basket full of party items and carried it with her instead of putting it on the moving van. The first night in their new home, out came the candleholders, the special plates and napkins, and the tablecloth—even though it had to be spread on the floor. Together, they celebrated being a family, having a new start in a new house, and God's faithfulness to them.

- *Staying in your house.* If you move frequently, you may want to celebrate living in the same house for more than a year. That's what we did. We celebrated with cake and candles, using a candle for each year we were in the same place.

- *Your child's or a friend's baptism.*

- *A special accomplishment or milestone.* Being inducted into an

CELEBRATING THE FIRSTS

"Mom, why do you always make cinnamon rolls when it snows?"

I thought for a moment. I wasn't sure how to explain it. "Oh, I don't know. It's just my way of celebrating the first snow."

"Why do you have to celebrate snow?"

"I don't have to do it, sweetie. I want to."

"Who taught you?"

"Your Grandma Lonnie did. She loved celebrating things.... When my sisters and I were growing up, she made sure we commemorated everything—the first fall leaf, the first spring leaf, the first lost tooth."[1]

—Shannon Woodward, *Homelife*

honors society, earning first chair in the clarinet section, getting a role in the school play, winning a conference title, or reaching a tough goal—all are calls for celebration.

- *A new job or promotion.* This can be quite significant, particularly if it has been a long time coming.

- *First things.* Your child's first bicycle ride without the training wheels, your older child's first day to drive the car, or your first solo at church can be great events to celebrate.

- *When school's out for the summer—and when it begins at summer's end.*

CELEBRATION TOOLS

- *Departure from routine.* Celebrations don't have to be fancy or expensive. They just need to be a break from the ordinary. Tablecloths, cloth napkins, stemmed glassware, candlelight, and special dishes all set the tone for a celebration. They announce "This is a special occasion!" Our family celebrated many a band performance and various swimming awards with M&M's and Pepsi. These were not everyday items at our house; they were a special treat.

  Some families signal a celebration with a certain object, such as a homemade crown or a special cup or plate. When that object appears, it says "Celebration time!" One family uses a certain goblet to toast special occasions. At first they used the goblet only for birthdays, Easter, and Christmas. Gradually, they began to use it to celebrate all sorts of family events: when good friends would visit or when one of them won a special honor or reached a goal. They fill the goblet, offer a toast for the honoree, then pass it from person to person for each to sip.

- *Create a celebration circle.* When the shepherd found his sheep, he called his friends and neighbors together and said, "I am so happy I found my lost sheep. Let us celebrate!" (Luke 15:6, TEV). When the woman found her lost coin, she, too, called her friends and neighbors together and said to them, "I am so happy I found the coin I lost. Let us celebrate!" (Luke 15:9, TEV). When the prodigal son returned home, his father said, "Let us celebrate with a feast!" (Luke 15:23, TEV). When we have reason to celebrate, we want to celebrate with our immediate family or a few close friends.

- *Words.* We should continually affirm our family members and friends, but sometimes the nuts and bolts of life distract us from doing so. Celebrations can remind us of what really matters. Our words don't have to be elaborate. "[They] can be as simple as holding up your lemonade glass and saying: 'To James—the best kickball player in kindergarten.' Or 'To Dad—the best hamburger grill cook this side of the Mississippi.' "[2]

CELEBRATE THE SPIRITUAL

Just as we celebrate physical, academic, and professional milestones, we can celebrate spiritual milestones.

- *Recognize your child's most important decision.* "When your child comes to tell you she trusted Jesus Christ as her Savior during Sunday school, join with the angels and rejoice!"[4] A spiritual birthday can be celebrated with a birthday party. Ask the guests to write a special blessing for the birthday person or to share a favorite Scripture passage. Present the guest of honor with a new Bible, inscribed with his or her name and date of conversion. Put a special sticker on the calendar, marking this important day.

• *Celebrate spiritual anniversaries.* One father makes a special date with his children on the anniversary of their conversion. He takes them to a favorite ice cream parlor, asks them about their walk with the Lord, and helps them think about how they want to grow in the coming year. A mother shares a Bible verse with her children on their spiritual anniversaries. She tells them that the verse will guide her prayers for them in the coming year.

• *Honor the Sabbath.* God commanded us to keep the Sabbath holy, distinctive from the other days of the week. Our family began every Sunday morning with a celebration breakfast of pancakes—served only on Sundays. With everybody up and at the table, we joined hands and said together, "This is the day that the LORD has made; let us rejoice and be glad in it" (Psalm 118:24, NIV). Our sons are grown now, but Bob and I still say, "This is the day that the Lord has made…" every Sunday morning. As we do so, we remember hundreds of

TELL THEM NOW

"I've learned a terrible truth from going to too many funerals in my life: So much of the praise comes after people are gone, in their eulogies. We ought to be telling them sooner. So I'm a big believer in toasting people at birthdays and anniversaries, family gatherings, special celebrations—toasting their great qualities, their friendship, their wisdom, their uniqueness. What could be better than being told out loud in a genuine way, with other people listening, that you are loved, respected, needed, appreciated, and adored?"[3]

—Maria Shriver, *Ten Things I Wish I'd Known Before I Went Out into the Real World*

LOOKING FOR THE GOOD—
AND CELEBRATING IT!

No one in my family had ever divorced. I assumed that marriage was for life. So when my wife and I divorced after five years of marriage and three years after the birth of our son, my world caved in. I was a failure in my own eyes.

I later remarried but confided to my wife, Fran, that I couldn't shake the feeling that my family life had failed. She asked me what was wrong with our family now (which included her daughter from a previous marriage and my son). I had to admit that, aside from the pain of being with my son only half the time (my ex-wife and I shared custody), our family life was wonderful.

"Then why don't you celebrate it?" she asked.[6]

—Dennis Prager, *Reader's Digest*

Sunday mornings when our family gathered, connected with one another and with God, and we trust God that our sons are continuing their heritage wherever they are.

- *Highlight God's work.* In Old Testament times, God's people often built memorials to remind them and their children of God's workings in their lives. Celebrations can also recognize God's work in our lives, giving us an opportunity to express our gratitude for all he does.

    One mother wrote, "When God provided a large and unexpected check from a relative, the kids came home to sparkling cider and donuts for their afternoon snack. We enjoyed a similar snack menu when Mom announced that she was expecting another baby. Only our son, Jonathan, had been praying for a baby brother, but this unexpected blessing was still a gift from God to be celebrated. Our kids now know God has done something great for our family when we break out the crystal glasses and bakery treats."[5]

THE OTHER SIDE OF CELEBRATION

When something special happens, we want to celebrate. But because celebrating lifts the spirit, celebrations can also help us cope during lackluster or difficult times. I first realized this at a time when money was tight and we were in transition.

My husband had finished graduate school. We had also just moved and were trying to adjust to a new place to call home. After the initial excitement of moving in had worn off, the days became dreary and lonely.

One afternoon when time seemed to lag and the children were restless, I got out a box of hand-me-down clothes that someone had given us. Jim was seven, Joel was five, and Ben was a baby. As we rummaged through the clothes, Jim and Joel found some sport coats just about their size and some white shirts and bow ties. I encouraged the boys to try them on. When they did, they looked at themselves in the mirror and thought they looked awfully handsome. I thought so too.

I looked at my watch then and realized it was about time for Bob to come home from work. I said to the boys, "Come on, let's go meet the bus." On the way out the door, on impulse I grabbed some flags.

When Bob stepped off the bus, there stood the four of us, Jim and Joel all dressed up, each of us waving a flag, and all of us singing, "For he's a jolly good fellow." Bob beamed.

We walked home together, hugging and laughing. We took a picture of ourselves. When Bob looks at that photo, he'll say, "That was a great day, wasn't it?" And it was. An ordinary day turned into an extraordinary one when we celebrated a father's coming home from work. The dreariness evaporated, joy returned, and a father felt appreciated.

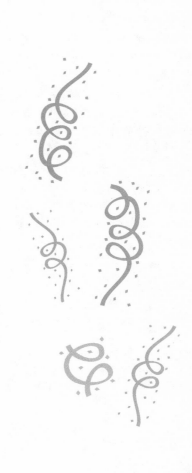

A TOUCH OF JOY

In the experience of a growing child the spirit of Christianity calls for a blending of love, joy, and serenity. In the words of grace before the family meal; in the few minutes of worship as a household, after the morning and the evening repast; above all, in the bedtime stories and the words of prayer before the good-night kiss, the dominant note should be that of joy. Such a home affords an object lesson of the heaven where some day the children of God are to be "lost in wonder, love and praise."[7]

—Andrew Watterson Blackwood,
This Year of Our Lord

Celebrations bring us closer to family, to friends, and to God. They help us put into words and actions the love that we feel and the values we hold, adding warmth and joy to our lives. So bang a drum, sing an anthem, march in a parade, or shout for joy. Express yourself, celebrate with meaning, and allow your heart to be touched!

NOTES

Chapter One

1. C. S. Lewis, *The Lion, the Witch, and the Wardrobe* (New York: Collier Books, Macmillan, 1950), 116.

Chapter Two

1. Phyllis Stanley and Miltinnie Yih, *Celebrate the Seasons* (Colorado Springs: NavPress, 1986), 41.
2. Juliana Sellers, as quoted in "From Our Readers," *FamilyFun,* February 2000, 42.
3. Marlene LeFever, *Parties with a Purpose* (Colorado Springs: Cook Ministry Resources, 1988), 230-7.
4. Wayne Rice and Mike Yaconelli, *Holiday Ideas for Youth Groups* (Grand Rapids, Mich.: Zondervan, 1981), 26.
5. Wicke Chambers and Spring Asher, *The Celebration Book of Great American Traditions* (New York: Harper & Row, 1983), 103.
6. Debbie Fick, "I Love You," *Virtue,* February/March 1999, 61. Used with the author's permission.
7. LeFever, *Parties,* 235.

Chapter Three

1. Leon McBeth, *Men Who Made Missions* (Nashville: Broadman, 1968), 17.
2. Martha Zimmerman, *Celebrating the Christian Year* (Minneapolis: Bethany, 1993), 121. Used with permission from Bethany House Publishers.

3. Zimmerman, *Christian Year,* 118-9.

4. McBeth, *Missions,* pages 18-9.

5. McBeth, *Missions,* 18.

6. Felice de Giardini, "Come, Thou Almighty King," *Hymnal for Boys and Girls* (Grand Rapids, Mich.: Singspiration, 1971), 28. The song is in the public domain.

7. Zimmerman, *Christian Year,* 122, and Francis X. Weiser, *The Holyday Book* (New York: Harcourt Brace, 1956), 155.

Chapter Four

1. Anne Class of Indianapolis, Indiana, shared this idea in a workshop on celebrating with meaning.

2. Patricia Machat, "Celebrating the Resurrection," *Discipleship Journal,* no. 62, 1991, 16.

3. Zimmerman, C*hristian Year,* 151. Used with permission from Bethany House Publishers.

4. I first read about these cookies in *HomeLife* magazine, April 1999, and the recipe is also available on the Internet. One source, http://ntl.sympatica.ca/~whogan/erec.htm, simply attributes the recipe to Tricia.

5. Kathryn Slattery, "How To: Make the Real Easter Real for Your Kids," *Guideposts,* April 1992, 19.

6. Alice van Straalen, *The Book of Holidays Around the World* (New York: Dutton, 1986), April.

7. Tee Billingsley, "Keeping Christ in Easter," *HomeLife,* April 1996, 48.

8. Jeanne Hunt, *Holy Bells and Wonderful Smells* (Cincinnati: St. Anthony Messenger Press, 1996), 77.

Chapter Five

1. James Muffett, "Faith of Our Founding Fathers," *Light and Life,* July-August 1998, 39.

2. Adapted from Robert Flood, *The Rebirth of America* (Bala Cynwyd, Pa.: Arthur S. DeMoss Foundation, 1986), 12.

3. Carol Barkin and Elizabeth James, *The Holiday Handbook* (New York: Clarion Books, 1994), 174.

4. Bernadette McCarver Snyder, *Saintly Celebrations and Holy Holidays* (Liguori, Mo.: Liguori, 1997), 63. Excerpt reprinted with permission of Liguori Publications, Liguori, MO 63057-9999. No other reproduction of this material is permitted.

5. The essay was a call for support of the World War II Savings Bonds and stamps used to finance the war. According to the *Times-Mail* of Bedford, Indiana, the source of the message was the U. S. Treasury Department, author unknown.

Chapter Six

1. Richard J. Foster, *Celebration of Discipline* (New York: Harper & Row, 1978), 170.

2. Zimmerman, *Christian Year,* 174-5. Used with permission from Bethany House Publishers.

3. Martin Hintz and Kate Hintz, *Halloween: Why We Celebrate It the Way We Do* (Mankato, Minn.: Capstone Press, 1996), 28, 31. Reprinted by permission of Capstone Press.

4. Irma S. Rombauer and Marion Rombauer Becker, *Joy of Cooking* (Indianapolis: Bobbs-Merrill, 1964), 605.

Chapter Seven

1. Snyder, *Saintly and Holy,* 101. Excerpt reprinted with permission of Liguori Publications, Liguori, MO 63057-9999. No other reproduction of this material is permitted.

2. Diana Karter Appelbaum, *Thanksgiving: An American Holiday, An American History* (New York: Facts on File, 1984), 25.

3. Variations of this idea also found in Gloria Gaither and Shirley Dobson, *Let's Make a Memory* (Nashville: Word, 1983) and Stanley and Yih, *Celebrate the Seasons.*

4. Karen O'Conner, *Basket of Blessings* (Colorado Springs: WaterBrook, 1998), 9.

5. Dag Hammarskjold, "Markings," trans. Leif Sjoberg and W. H. Auden (New York: Knopf; London: Faber and Faber, 1964), originally published as "Vagmarken" (Stockholm: Albert Bonniers Forlag AB, 1963).

6. Lettie Kirkpatrick, "Giving Thanks," *Christian Parenting Today,* November/December 1999, 54.

7. Hunt, *Holy and Wonderful,* 14. Reprinted by permission of St. Anthony Messenger Press, 1615 Republic Street, Cincinnati, OH 45210. All rights reserved.

CHAPTER EIGHT

1. The Schroeder Family, *Celebrate While We Wait* (St. Louis, Mo.: Concordia, 1977), 4. Used with the author's permission.

2. Sue Monk Kidd, "How To: Stop, Look, and Listen for Christmas," *Guideposts,* December 1986, 18-9. Reprinted with permission from *Guideposts Magazine* (December 1986). Copyright © 1986 by Guideposts, Carmel, New York 10512.

3. Evelyn Christenson, *What Happens When We Pray for Our Families* (Wheaton, Ill.: Victor, 1992), 181. © 1992 Cook Communications Ministries. Copied with permission. May not be further reproduced. All rights reserved.

4. Jan Dargatz, "Advent Anticipation," *Virtue,* November/December 1991, 81. Used with permission.

5. Beverly Thompson, "The Christmas Tree That Grew…and Grew…and Grows," *Guideposts,* December 1994, 19.

6. Helen E. Siml, "How to Make a New Kind of Advent Calendar," *Christian Life,* November 1981, 49-50. Used with permission.

CHAPTER NINE

1. Advent originated in the fourth century as a period of penance and of preparation for baptisms at Epiphany (January 6).

2. Adapted from Catherine Brandt, *We Light the Candles* (Minneapolis: Augsburg, 1976).

3. Adapted from Sally M. Jarvis, quoted in Patricia and Donald Griggs, *Teaching and Celebrating Advent* (Nashville: Abingdon, 1980), 8.

4. Adapted from Jan Johnson, "Making Christmas Special—From Jan," in Christenson, *Pray For Our Families,* 181-2.

5. Adapted from "A Plan for Celebrating Advent," *Decision,* December 1998, 11.

6. T. G. Crippen, *Christmas and Christmas Lore* (Detroit: Gale Research Company, 1971), 114.

7. Howard A. Whaley, "How We Did It," *Moody,* December 1979, 27.

8. Schroeder, *While We Wait,* 4-5.

9. Adapted from LeFever, *Parties,* 221-2.

10. Mercedes Andrei, quoted in Lindy Warren, "Christmas Moments that Matter," *Virtue,* November/December 1992, 39.

CHAPTER TEN

1. I would like to credit the originator of this finger play, but I don't know who it is. When my sons Jim and Joel were preschoolers, the children's workers at our church taught this to them.

2. Schroeder, *While We Wait,* 6. Used with the author's permission.

3. Gordon Greer, "Editor at Large," *Better Homes and Gardens,* December 1982, 2.

4. "Including Young and Old," *Visitations,* December 1991, 11.

5. Lillian Daniel, "I Love to Tell the Story to Those Who Know It Least," *Christianity Today,* August 9, 1999, 50.

6. Used with the author's permission.

7. Used with the author's permission.

Chapter Eleven

1. Jane Belk Moncure, *Our Mother's Day Book* (Elgin, Ill.: The Child's World, 1987), 17.

2. Barbara Baumgardner, "The Ultimate Greeting Card," *Virtue,* December 1998/January 1999, 34. Used with the author's permission.

3. Franny Shuker-Haines, "Father's Day Memory Game," *Children's Television Workshop,* May 27, 2000. Found at http://www.ctw.org.

4. Mary Kay Phelan, *Mother's Day* (New York: Thomas Y. Crowell Company, 1965), 24.

5. Shelly Nielsen, *Celebrating Mother's Day* (Edina, Minn.: Abdo & Daughters, 1996), 23. Reprinted with permission.

6. Moncure, *Mother's Day Book,* 19.

7. Shelly Nielsen, *Celebrating Father's Day* (Edina, Minn.: Abdo & Daughters, 1996), 25.

8. Hunt, *Holy and Wonderful,* 98. Reprinted by permission of St. Anthony Messenger Press, 1615 Republic Street, Cincinnati, OH 45210. All rights reserved.

Chapter Twelve

1. Luci Swindoll, *You Bring the Confetti, God Brings the Joy* (Dallas: Word, 1986), 36.

2. Gaither and Dobson, *Make a Memory,* 67.

3. Holly W. Whitcomb, *Feasting with God* (Cleveland: United Church Press, 1996), 84.

4. Christenson, *Pray for Our Families,* 178-9. © 1992 Cook Communications Ministries. Copied with permission. May not be further reproduced. All rights reserved.

5. Philip Gulley, *For Everything a Season* (Sisters, Oreg.: Multnomah, 1999), 15.

CHAPTER THIRTEEN

1. Swindoll, *Confetti,* 115.

2. Hunt, *Holy and Wonderful,* 111. Reprinted by permission of St. Anthony Messenger Press, 1615 Republic Street, Cincinnati, OH 45210. All rights reserved.

3. Carol Kuykendall, "Celebrating Your High School Graduate," *Parents of Teenagers,* May/June 1994, 11.

4. Elie Wiesel, "Have You Learned the Most Important Lesson of All?" *Parade Magazine,* May 24, 1992, 4.

CHAPTER FOURTEEN

1. Harold and Bette Gillogly, "A Passion for Oneness," *HomeLife,* February 2000, 26.

2. Jacqueline Smith, *The Creative Wedding Idea Book* (Holbrook, Mass.: Bob Adams, 1994), 172.

3. Sydney Barbara Metrick, *I Do: A Guide to Creating Your Own Unique Wedding Ceremony* (Berkeley, Calif.: Celestial Arts, 1992), 99.

4. Migon McLaughlin, quoted in Smith, *Wedding Idea Book,* 201.

5. Judith Viorst, "Honor Thy Marriage (and Anniversary)," *Redbook,* June 1990, 48.

6. Francine Klagsbrun, "What Really Makes a Marriage Work," *Reader's Digest,* October 1985, 89.

7. Cynthia Lueck Sowden, *An Anniversary to Remember* (St. Paul, Minn.: Brighton, 1992), 51.

8. Rayburn W. Ray and Rose Ann Ray, *Wedding Anniversary Idea Book* (Brentwood, Tenn.: JM Publications, 1985), 41, 78.

9. Ray and Ray, *Anniversary Idea Book,* 78-9.

10. Used with permission.

11. Sowden, *Anniversary to Remember,* 85.

12. Neno O'Neill, "Fifty Years of Love," *Reader's Digest,* November 1979, 192.

Chapter Fifteen

1. Shannon Woodward, "Heirlooms," *HomeLife,* January 1999, 24.

2. Kathy Peel, "Cement Your Family with Celebrations!" *Virtue,* May/June 1993, 26.

3. Maria Shriver, *Ten Things I Wish I'd Known Before I Went Out into the Real World* (New York: Warner Books, Inc., 2000), 123-4.

4. Renee S. Sanford, "Celebrating Your Steps Toward God," *HomeLife,* March 1999, 45.

5. Sanford, "Celebrating," 45.

6. Dennis Prager, "A Simple Truth About Happiness," *Reader's Digest,* June 1998, 98-9. Originally appeared in Dennis Prager, *Happiness Is a Serious Problem* (New York: Harper-Collins, 1998), 27-8. Reprinted with permission from the June 1998 Reader's Digest.

7. Andrew Watterson Blackwood, *This Year of Our Lord* (Philadelphia: Westminster, 1943), 156.

SELECTED BIBLIOGRAPHY

Appelbaum, Diana Karter. *Thanksgiving: An American Holiday, An American History.* New York: Facts on File Publications, 1984.

Barkin, Carol, and Elizabeth James. *The Holiday Handbook.* New York: Clarion Books, 1994.

Barta, Stacie Hill. *Wacky Cakes and Water Snakes.* New York: Penguin Books, 1995.

Berg, Elizabeth. *Family Traditions: Celebrations for Holidays and Everyday.* Pleasantville, N.Y.: *Reader's Digest,* 1992.

Billingsley, Tee. "Keeping Christ in Easter." *HomeLife,* April 1996.

Christenson, Evelyn. *What Happens When We Pray for Our Families.* Wheaton, Ill.: Victor Books, 1992.

Dargatz, Jan. "Advent Anticipation." *Virtue,* November/December 1991.

Diller, Harriett. *Celebrations That Matter: A Year-round Guide to Making Holidays Meaningful.* Minneapolis: Augsburg Fortress, 1990.

Ebert, Linda. "A Family Easter Celebration." *Virtue,* March/April 1990.

Fulghum, Robert. *From Beginning to End.* New York: Villard Books, 1995.

Gaither, Gloria, and Shirley Dobson. *Let's Make a Memory.* Dallas: Word, 1983.

Gordon, Anita. "Sprucing Up Your Family's Christmas." *Focus on the Family* magazine, December 1987.

Hibbard, Ann. *Family Celebrations at Easter.* Grand Rapids, Mich.: A Raven's Ridge Book, Baker Books, 1994.

Hunt, Jeanne. *Holy Bells and Wonderful Smells.* Cincinnati: St. Anthony Messenger Press, 1996.

Krueger, Caryl. *The Family Party Book.* Nashville: Abingdon, 1996.

Kuykendall, Carol. "Celebrating Your High School Graduate." *Parents of Teenagers,* May/June 1994.

Lieberman, Susan A. *New Traditions: Redefining Celebrations for Today's Family.* New York: Farrar, Straus & Giroux, Inc., 1991.

LeFever, Marlene D. *Parties with a Purpose.* Colorado Springs: Cook Ministry Resources, 1988.

Machat, Patricia. "Celebrating the Resurrection." *Discipleship Journal,* no. 62, 1991.

Metrick, Sydney Barbara. *I Do: A Guide to Creating Your Own Unique Wedding Ceremony.* Berkeley, Calif.: Celestial Arts, 1992.

Moncure, Jane Belk. *Our Mother's Day Book.* Elgin, Ill.: The Child's World, 1987.

Nielsen, Shelly. *Celebrating Father's Day.* Edina, Minn.: Abdo & Daughters, 1996.

O'Neill, Neno. "Fifty Years of Love." *Reader's Digest,* November 1979.

Peel, Kathy. "Cement Your Family with Celebrations!" *Virtue,* May/June 1993.

Sanford, Renee S. "Celebrating Your Steps Toward God." *HomeLife,* March 1999.

The Schroeder Family. *Celebrate While We Wait.* St. Louis, Mo.: Concordia, 1977.

Siml, Helen E. "How to Make a New Kind of Advent Calendar." *Christian Life,* November 1981.

Slattery, Kathryn. "How To: Make the Real Easter Real for Your Kids." *Guideposts,* April 1992.

Smith, Jacqueline. *The Creative Wedding Idea Book.* Holbrook, Mass.: Bob Adams, Inc., 1994.

Snyder, Bernadette McCarver. *Saintly Celebrations and Holy Holidays.* Liguori, Mo.: Liguori Publications, 1997.

Sowden, Cynthia Lueck. *An Anniversary to Remember.* St. Paul, Minn.: Brighton Publications, Inc., 1992.

Stanley, Phyllis, and Miltinnie Yih. *Celebrate the Seasons.* Colorado Springs: NavPress, 1986.

Swindoll, Luci. *You Bring the Confetti, God Brings the Joy.* Dallas: Word, 1986.

Thomas, Dian. *Holiday Fun Year-Round with Dian Thomas.* Holladay, Utah: The Dian Thomas Company, 1995.

Viorst, Judith. "Honor Thy Marriage (and Anniversary)." *Redbook,* June 1990.

Warren, Lindy. "Christmas Moments that Matter." *Virtue,* December 1992.

Whitcomb, Holly W. *Feasting with God.* Cleveland: United Church Press, 1996.

Zimmerman, Martha. *Celebrating the Christian Year.* Minneapolis: Bethany, 1993.

———. *Celebrate the Feasts.* Minneapolis: Bethany, 1993.